on track ...
Procol
Harum

every album, every song

Scott Meze

sonicbondpublishing.com

Sonicbond Publishing Limited
www.sonicbondpublishing.co.uk
Email: info@sonicbondpublishing.co.uk

First Published in the United Kingdom 2024
First Published in the United States 2024

British Library Cataloguing in Publication Data:
A Catalogue record for this book is available from the British Library

Copyright Scott Meze 2024

ISBN 978-1-78952-315-7

Typeset in ITC Garamond Std & ITC Avant Garde Gothic
Printed and bound in England

Graphic design and typesetting: Full Moon Media

Follow us on social media:
Twitter: https://twitter.com/SonicbondP
Instagram: www.instagram.com/sonicbondpublishing_/
Facebook: www.facebook.com/SonicbondPublishing/

Linktree QR code:

on track ...
Procol Harum

Contents

Would you like to write for Sonicbond Publishing?

At Sonicbond Publishing we are always on the look-out for authors, particularly for our two main series:

On Track. Mixing fact with in depth analysis, the On Track series examines the work of a particular musical artist or group. All genres are considered from easy listening and jazz to 60s soul to 90s pop, via rock and metal.

On Screen. This series looks at the world of film and television. Subjects considered include directors, actors and writers, as well as entire television and film series. As with the On Track series, we balance fact with analysis.

While professional writing experience would, of course, be an advantage the most important qualification is to have real enthusiasm and knowledge of your subject. First-time authors are welcomed, but the ability to write well in English is essential.

Sonicbond Publishing has distribution throughout Europe and North America, and all books are also published in E-book form. Authors will be paid a royalty based on sales of their book.

Further details are available from www.sonicbondpublishing.co.uk. To contact us, complete the contact form there or
email info@sonicbondpublishing.co.uk

Introduction

The passing of Procol Harum's mentors and main shapers in 2022 and 2023 left us with a room that seems perpetually half-painted. There are so many mysteries about the band that we might have wanted Gary Brooker (their principal songwriter) and Keith Reid (their principal lyricist) to have explained for us. And yet, though many interviewers questioned them over the more than half-century that the band existed, we never did fully unlock the mysteries, and now we never shall.

What's left is a series of paradoxes. Procol Harum erupted into life – an unexpected brilliance that turned the world magically technicolour overnight – at the very pinnacle of pop's climb from ephemera to everlasting craft. Witness the fact we're still talking about their debut single all these decades later, though I bet you couldn't name the song it dislodged from the top of the British charts. But afterwards, the industry turned its back on the band, refusing to allow them to build on that success. 'A Whiter Shade Of Pale' was as transformative as *Sgt. Pepper's Lonely Hearts Club Band* (released just two weeks later), but unlike The Beatles, Procol Harum are ossified forever in that moment: trapped in the single's grooves. They went on to create an extensive body of music – sometimes elaborate and elegant, sometimes raucous and unpretentious – that is revered by both pop and rock fans, and yet they've mostly been ignored by the press. Their career was laced with further songs that should have been hits and somehow weren't. They had a dignified, regal image, even when Reid wrote and Brooker sang some of the earthiest of all rock lyrics. They seemed funereal and stuffy despite a succession of squalling blues guitarists and a drummer who whipped up a sonic emotional storm. They pioneered and perfected the busting of the barriers that divided lowbrow pop from highbrow classical music, prompting countless less-adept bands to do the same. And yet there's still something haughty about the prog-rock crowd's reaction to Procol Harum: not quite symphonic enough, it seems, not nearly enough flash.

There have been other singular groups in rock, those whose individual paths took them outside the mainstream of their genre. In particular, I'm thinking of Pink Floyd – a band with which Brooker identified and which shared a pioneering spirit – or those like King Crimson and Van der Graaf Generator, who found longevity and successive generations of audiences through a sound inimitable and odd. It's among these maverick artists and fierce visionaries that Procol Harum find their place.

'I sat me down to write a simple story', Reid wrote. So did I, at least for those whose interest in the band is fixed forever in 1967. On the surface, *that* band's trajectory is distinguishable enough from others who were likewise forged in the crucible of the early 1960s, who rose to fame in the countercultural ferments of the end of that decade, and who then sputtered for years before achieving rehabilitation on the legacy circuit. (The style is a *little* different, but this is the way we now receive Jefferson Airplane, for example.) It's simple because many listeners care only about 'Pale' (the abbreviation Brooker used, and so the one I shall, too) and disregard the rest. Say the words 'Procol Harum' to all but a small subset of those who recognize the name, and the song leaps out like a knee-jerk reaction. The unfortunate truth is that the band always *were* reduced to 'Pale'. Whatever they did afterwards, you can guarantee that any article on the band or its members will mention 'Pale', probably as some witty reference in the headline. Here, then, is the immovable object against which this book heaves and it's bound to fail to budge it an inch. Procol Harum: one hit wonders. What else is there to fill these pages with?

Look closer, and the story's not simple at all. The band recorded well over 150 *other* songs, sometimes in multiple versions, and released them on 12 studio albums, as many again official live albums, and a baffling array of compilations and one-offs. The tale all this work tells is of a band that thought they'd conquered the pop single on their first attempt (and you don't get to brag unless you've conquered quite as demonstrably as 'Pale' did) and no longer had anything to prove there, helping to kick-start album-orientated rock in the process. (The Moody Blues were immediate followers, from which much else sprang.) They longed for more hits but only to attract a wider audience for the rest of their material. Among Procol Harum's run of six peak albums from 1968 to 1973 are *Shine On Brightly*, an album at least partly responsible for heavy metal and prog rock, *A Salty Dog*, the band's brine-soaked masterpiece, and the aching, scarifying, lost soul howling of *Home*. And yet – there's just that one song, right?

Of course, I'm going to cover 'Pale' in detail because this may be why you're here. But if I've done my job correctly, by the end of the book, you'll have forgotten it altogether. You may even agree with me that the band's best work came later, that their finest albums accumulate into sound worlds much more powerful and accomplished than their rather clunky debut single, that Gary Brooker matured into a better singer and songwriter, and that the band's determination to elevate themselves grew from a collision of extraordinary talent pushing hard against the sheer unyielding bulk of *that song*. In short, that they succeeded again and again, even if the press had no interest in listening.

As for Keith Reid – whose mysterious verses fuelled innumerable theories (and who was careful never to disprove any of them), there's far more to admire than just light fandangos and vestal virgins. It's true he simplified his words and lost most of his early power as his career progressed, but this is still the man who gave us some of rock's most startling and poetic phrases – including lines like 'Dull and sullen, much subdued/My skull a stony glaze', 'Keeping watch on smoking cinders', 'Whose perfumed depths sing songs of gloom', and 'A river of tears and an ocean of pain'. Bob Dylan was an early influence, but Dylan couldn't maintain poetry so penetrating. Reid's lines are firecrackers thrown in dark halls. They illuminate and frighten in equal measure.

For sure, the book is an elegy for the members we lost recently, and as much as possible, I have tried to tell it in their words. But it's also a riotous send-off for what may seem like the most reserved of pleasures. Here's one more Reid quote: 'Our fortunes speed, and dissipate'. No, Keith, not here, they don't.

Gary Brooker And The Roots Of Procol Harum

A seaside resort easily accessible from London, Southend-on-Sea in Essex hosted a constant influx of holidaymakers and, crucially, their bored teenage children who wanted more than just amusement parks and pleasure piers. In the early-1960s, you could make a living there playing covers of the US hits of the day. Local band The Paramounts – whose members variously included Gary Brooker on piano and vocals, Robin Trower and Chris Copping on guitar, and Barrie James (B.J.) Wilson on drums – also benefited from a friendship with DJ Guy Stevens, who supplied them with new American sounds before they'd been covered by other British bands.

The Paramounts soon outgrew the town and began confident journeys into London. EMI showed interest, signing them to Parlophone for six singles between 1963 and 1965, though only the first – 'Poison Ivy' (a US hit for The Coasters) – gained much traction. But as British pop changed around The Paramounts (a precipitous ascent through mod and folk rock toward the first intimations of psychedelia in 1966), they found themselves rudderless. They slipped into anonymity and ceased working altogether in the middle of 1966. Brooker found himself an unemployed 21-year-old professional musician at a point in time when swinging London was bursting into life all around him. Things were bright for someone of his abilities. But he was exhausted from years of touring and had no intention of putting himself back on the pop treadmill.

It was a complex calculation. Brooker knew that piano was the sound of the moment. Within intricate arrangements by The Beatles and The Beach Boys, it added quasi-classical depth and grandeur to what was (even as early as 1966) beginning to be called 'progressive' pop music. In the decade to come, it was the piano that would propel soulful white singer-songwriters such as Elton John and Billy Joel to fame – a role Brooker could have feasibly claimed for himself. And like many of those progressive artists of his generation, Brooker was poised between an appreciation for the sophistication of classical music and a love of the pure power and energy of rock.

As a kid, he'd never taken serious lessons and never put himself through music school. Nor was he quite as classically educated as the Procol Harum songs suggest. Brooker admitted to the *New Musical Express* in 1972: 'I've never listened to much classical music, not at all in fact. I know the theme from *2001*, 'Sugar Plum Fairy' and a couple of Bach things, 'Moonlight Sonata'. But that's about as far as my knowledge goes'. He preferred the immediacy and emotional connection of soul singers like Sam Cooke and Ray Charles to formal classical music: a man at a piano accompanying gospel-inflected outpourings of emotion. It helped that he had the rich, thickly nasal intonation to pull off the style (a *black* voice, reductively). He told *Contemporary Keyboard* in 1978:

> We had a piano at home, and my father was a musician. I got sent off to
> take piano lessons when I was about five. I didn't get on with the practising

part. I'd rather play tunes that I wanted to play instead of Schumann's *Humoresque* or something like that. After my father died, I stopped playing for a good couple of years. Then a friend of my father's gave me two years of piano lessons as a present, so off I went again to try and learn. This teacher was much better, though. He taught you to play tunes you wanted to learn. I liked 'Deep Purple', so he'd write it down and I'd learn it. You learn more about the song and its chord structure that way, so instead of just learning notes from a piece of paper, I was finding out more about how a song was constructed.

By 1966, Brooker knew enough of the theory of music to move his fingers onto more than the standard handful of chords on which pop and soul had been built: to look further than the obvious. His taste in music was also evolving to match the times. Even if he wasn't *quite* ready to emulate The Left Banke (whose Procol-intimating single 'Walk Away Renée' was released in July), he *did* latch onto The Young Rascals. That February, their 'Good Lovin'' popularised an upbeat rock-belter style with blue-eyed soul croons thickened by swells of organ. When Procol Harum shot to fame in 1967, Brooker was happy to tell the press that The Young Rascals were his favourite group. Still, he never abandoned the piano, never played tricky Hammond runs, never shifted into experimenting with synths and other voices, even in his later years when he'd package a synthesizer inside a mock grand piano shell on stage. In 1978, *Contemporary Keyboard* magazine asked him if piano was the only instrument he played with Procol Harum. Brooker replied:

> Yeah, except for electric piano on one or two tracks. I played other instruments on 'Song For A Dreamer' and 'Memorial Drive'. I played string bass on 'Barnyard Story', with chalk marks on the neck to show where the frets would be. And I strummed the acoustic guitar quite a bit on *A Salty Dog*, on *Home*, and there's guitar on 'Beyond The Pale'. And there are some balalaika bits. I've played rhythm guitar onstage on occasion. I played (organ) onstage once. The organist and I used to swap over for a couple of numbers.

And that was it: mostly piano all the way. But there was more to his inspiration than just the soul pianists of his youth. On The Young Rascals' first album (released in March 1966), there was a cover of Bob Dylan's 'Like A Rolling Stone': a near-facsimile, right down to the vocal intonations. Much of what Brooker began to formulate in 1966 – as heard on the first Procol Harum album – shows the distinct influence of Dylan's two 1965 albums, *Bringing It All Back Home* and *Highway 61 Revisited*. That a style based directly on these models was the plan was revealed in the advertisement Brooker placed in *Melody Maker* on 28 January 1967, soliciting members for a 'new project with Y. Rascals/Dylan type sound'.

But that was the future. In the waning months of 1966, Brooker thought he could be a non-performing songwriter. And to emulate even a token of Dylan's compelling strengths, Brooker needed to find himself a lyricist.

Enter Keith Reid, Dragging A Coffin

Early in 1966, while The Paramounts were still struggling on and long before Brooker realised he would have to make it on his own, Guy Stevens introduced him to a would-be poet who was trying to break into songwriting. Brooker recalled the circumstances of the meeting to UCLA Radio in 2001:

> One day, he said: 'This is Keith Reid. He writes words'. And I said: 'Oh, really? I've never written music before. Why would I want to do that when there's all this good stuff around to play?' But I remember being handed a bag full of his lyrics. In fact, I think I went home stoned and didn't find it until quite some months later. There was a vague recollection of where I got it, and when I opened it up, I think there were about ten lyrics in there, which were absolutely marvellous. And as soon as I read them, I sat down and wrote a song with the first one.

For *Sounds* in 1971, he added:

> I went to the piano and, for the first time in my life, composed a song. The words had to do with a tombstone following Keith around. I didn't discover until afterwards that these were the first words he'd written. That same afternoon, I received a letter from Keith. It asked me to ring him and closed with a line from the words he'd written about the tombstone. We spoke and decided to work together.

That song, 'Something Following Me', became the template for all that followed: a sly, enigmatic tale of a man pursued – a little comically but with fierce intensity – by his own inescapable death.

Reid also asserted that this was his first song. In 1969, he told *Crawdaddy* magazine that the song was 'the first song lyric I wrote', by which I take it he means the first set of words that became a finished professional song. It may just as easily have meant that Reid sent Brooker some very old and much-rejected work. 'Something Following Me' was certainly not the first time Reid had heard his words set to music. In his teens, he'd tried writing songs with neighbour Marc Feld (later Marc Bolan). More recently, Reid had given two lyrics to singer Michel Polnareff – 'Time Will Tell' and 'You'll Be On My Mind' – which were released on Polnareff's French-chart-topping album *Love Me, Please Love Me* in spring, 1966.

That Brooker and Reid hit it off is surprising, given their quite different experiences in the industry. Brooker had had some minor success in The Paramounts, including appearing on *Ready, Steady Go!* and playing a couple of dates supporting The Beatles. Reid – who was just over a year younger than him – had practically nothing to show for himself in his home country. The closest he came to a breakthrough was when he managed to get a sheaf of lyrics to Steve Winwood of The Spencer Davis Group, but Reid recalled

11

that that band's lyricist Jim Capaldi ensured that Reid was muscled out. There was even a chance that Reid might write for the newly formed Cream, but Pete Brown got *that* gig.

Reid's bookish and somewhat severe look was never likely to make him a frontman, even if he'd wanted to be (though it *was* possible, as Robert Fripp demonstrated), so instead, he positioned himself as a Coleridge of the suburbs, charting macabre seas of the imagination. Reid never seemed to like to talk openly about himself and may well have dissembled just how scholarly he really was. For example, he told *The Argotist* in 2008: 'I never read any poetry at school. I never really read any poetry until sometime in the '90s'. He also admitted to failing his eleven-plus and being an academic washout. 'I wasn't any good at academic work', he told *The Times* of London in 1972. But in *The Daily Express* in 1997, he spun quite a different tale:

> My mother taught me to read at a very early age when I was about four or so, and I read constantly and voraciously until I left school when I was 15. I'd go to Mile End Library. My parents let me use their ticket, so I used to go not just into the children's library but upstairs in the grown-up's library as well. I just used to grab anything off the shelf that looked interesting. It was my escape, really. I escaped into a world of books.

And for sure, his work is peppered with classical allusions, as well as the Biblical references you'd expect of a Jewish poet steeped in introspection. Reid proudly noted that while he was working in the city as a legal clerk, he'd pop over to Foyles bookshop at lunchtime and immerse himself in literature. Thus inspired, he'd secretly write lyrics at his desk.

In *Crawdaddy* in 1970, Brooker noted the enigma at the heart of Reid's quasi-academic approach to writing: 'In 'Pilgrim's Progress', I'd never read the book of the same name – by John Bunyan, isn't it? – and I read what must have been the preface, and it was exactly the same tone as Keith's words. So I said to him, 'Have you read this?' and he said 'No'. And it was exactly the same. Not the same words, but the same tone'.

What Reid certainly *did* have by the time he began writing songs with Brooker was a mutual appreciation for another Jewish poet steeped in introspection: Bob Dylan. Reid told UCLA Radio in 2002: 'Without question, Bob Dylan was a huge influence on me, right at the beginning. He was the first person that when I heard him, I thought, 'Hmm, maybe I could do that'. So although I'd liked a lot of music and liked a lot of songs before then, it was Dylan that made me think I could write'.

By and large, Brooker and Reid's working technique wouldn't alter from their first days together in 1966 to the sundering of their professional relationship after *The Well's On Fire* in 2003. According to Reid, the lyric tended to come first. He'd post it to Brooker, and Brooker would feel his way around the piano until he'd invented a way to frame it into a song. Reid told *Goldmine* in 2009:

His method was basically to sit down at the piano and put some lyrics up there and just play around with some chords, see if anything fit. And then if he'd get an idea, get a spark of something, he'd give me a call and say: 'I think I've got something which will maybe work with this. Why don't you come and have a listen and see what you think?'. We'd get together and he'd play me sort of bits and pieces, and I'd say, 'Oh yeah, I think that works well. Why don't you maybe go somewhere here or go somewhere there?' or 'I think we've got it'. We'd just generally have these kinds of songwriting sessions and pull the songs together.

The place the two men's versions of events differed markedly is that often Brooker would already have a tune, and would look for a Reid lyric to fit it. Brooker told *SongwriterUniverse* in 2020: 'I'd have ideas sitting at the piano, just waiting for the right thing to come along. And that's the way it happened most times. There is an idea I would have, and suddenly, there was a lyric there that was perfect. Because I was a singer, I could vocalise, so you can make any lyric fit your musical lines because you're singing it. So the phrasing is up to me'.

Phrasing aside, Brooker wouldn't mess too much with the words, choosing instead to develop lyrics or reject them wholesale based on whether he thought they suited him. In 2018, he told *Prog* magazine: 'I always had a whole folder of Reid's lyrics that didn't get used. Sometimes the idea was too brief, and I couldn't fit it into something, or it didn't spur an idea. Now and again, there would be something I liked, but there would be some words in it that I just couldn't sing. Sometimes Reid just said, 'Oh, okay', and didn't try to change it. So it never got done'.

Reid's resistance to change the lyrics as originally written seems to have caused the most friction between the two men. During the press rounds for *Novum* – the only Procol Harum album written with Pete Brown – Brooker stressed how great it was to finally work with a lyricist who didn't mind if you asked for rewrites. Still, once the song was in progress, the pair worked it up to a finished state together, as Reid told *Zigzag* in 1973: 'I always know what it's like before we go in and record it. That's the strength or weakness of the relationship, you know. The better the words and music come together, the more perfect the marriage, the better the song. The most successful songs we do are the best marriages of words and music'.

Like Dylan in 1965, Reid's lyrics were often opaque to everyone else. Certainly, Brooker had little clue as to their true meaning. Though Reid's work became less painterly and more direct in 1971 when he shifted his allegiance from Dylan to Randy Newman, the abiding feel of early Procol Harum is of a mysterious dreamlike suspension in which everyday objects and events are transformed not so much into drug-like states but into that unsteady and somewhat queasy liminal space between hard reality and the tricks of the subconscious – the surrealism of Giorgio de Chirico or Leonora

Carrington placed in contemporary urban settings. Reid admitted to being influenced by painters, in particular Francis Bacon. Much of this early work is dark, haunted and subtly menacing, and it's no surprise that almost from the start, Reid equated emotional states – especially those of feeling lost, heartbroken, or afraid – with Coleridge-like voyages on bottomless black seas.

There's as strong a moral centre throughout Reid's lyrics as there is in Dylan's. Reid told *Creem* in 1972: 'There's no bleak attitude, no death attitude. I'm not on a death trip or anything. It's only realistic. The thing is, it doesn't matter how horrific anything is. It's not negative. It's not nice to stick a bayonet in someone's stomach. But it's not a negative action. It's a wrong action'.

Since these lyrics were part of what made Procol Harum so distinctive, they've often been the focus of interview questions. Reid obliged in trying to shine at least a little light on his motivations, even if the songs themselves usually remained out of our grasp. For instance, he told *Street Life* in 1976: 'They're not intended to be immediately accessible. I like images. I like evoking moods. I don't think I should provide some sort of detailed commentary on each set of words, exactly what I had in mind at the time of writing. A large part of a song's effect lies in how it seems to different people'.

In *Goldmine* in 2021, Brooker agreed: 'I could usually throw myself into Keith's words. They never sounded weird to me. I mean, there are a few exceptions, but I don't mind a bit of blood and gore. I can get through that. I'm not going to growl it out like Alice Cooper would. But you've got to make people feel there are nasty things out there as well. If you could do that, then you've done a little bit of your job'. Besides, even in the Gothic depths of Reid's obsessions with death and rot, he could always lighten the mood with humour – even sex, as we'll see.

Having bonded in their ability to turn words and fragments of tunes into songs, Brooker and Reid became an enduring partnership, creating well over 70 songs for Procol Harum. In November 1967, Brooker gave *Beat Instrumental* a clue to what made them tick: 'He writes the most beautiful lyrics. Setting them to music is a joy. Sometimes, he just stands there and reads aloud a new set of words, and we're spellbound'.

But in 1966, the pair's plan was to farm out their songs to established artists. In 1976, *Zigzag* quoted Brooker about these attempts: 'I took our songs along to a few contacts from the days of The Paramounts, like Andrew Oldham, who paid for a demo with just me at the piano. But we didn't have any luck at all. We got a definite elbow. I thought the numbers were all right, but nobody was at all interested in doing them'.

When they failed to find a single taker (with hindsight, it's hard to imagine The Beach Boys singing 'Conquistador' as intended), Brooker reluctantly conceded that he'd need to reform his band to perform them. That decision seems to have come at the beginning of 1967, given the 28 January *Melody*

Maker advert. The Paramounts had long scattered. Robin Trower now had his own band in Southend-on-Sea called The Jam. Though Brooker tried a few demos with B.J. Wilson, the drummer wasn't interested in coming back on board. Bassist Diz Derrick had given up music altogether. So Brooker and Reid brainstormed the kind of band they'd want around them (which, unsurprisingly, was one with the same kind of lineup as The Young Rascals, complete with stinging blues guitar and organ to complement Brooker's piano) and began accumulating personnel. Brooker told *Shindig* in 2018: 'The only thing I was fixed on was that as well as the usual guitar/bass/drums lineup and myself on electric piano, we would have a Hammond organ too'.

The choice of band name was decisively settled by Guy Stevens. He had a friend who bred pedigree Blue Burmese cats. One male cat was named Procul Harun, which Stevens either mistakenly transcribed as Procol Harum or purposefully softened to sound less Arabic. (Reid may also have had a hand in this, given the sentiments he expressed in the song 'Poor Mohammed' much later.) Either way, it was to be the source of abiding confusion, especially given that those misled by a little classical education thought it should be the Latin 'procul earum', hence meaning 'far from them' or words to that effect. In fact, it's nothing of the sort. The breeder's identifier name for their cats was Procul, and for a 1964 litter, they chose the given names Harun, Hussein, and Lady Sonia.

It was at this point that Brooker and Reid's fortunes finally began to change. Through Reid's contacts, they gained back-end support: Denny Cordell and David Platz to handle the music and Jonathan Weston to manage the group. By the time of the *Melody Maker* advert, they'd built up a roster of worthwhile demos – essentially the same repertoire that was to form the band's first UK album. And squirrelled away in their back pockets was the song that would change everything.

'A Whiter Shade Of Pale' (Single) (1967)

Personnel:
Gary Brooker: piano, vocals
Bill Eyden: drums
Matthew Fisher: organ
David Knights: bass
Written by: Brooker, Fisher, Reid
Recorded: March 1967, Olympic Studios, London, UK
Producer: Denny Cordell
Label: Deram
Release date: May 1967
Charts: UK: 1, US: 5
Length: 3:59

As I mentioned in the introduction, many of those who pick up this book are here for one thing only. True, it's a pretty big thing. 'A Whiter Shade Of Pale' is deeply embedded in the collective consciousness not just of those who lived through a specific period of time (the Summer of Love) but of those who discovered it later and embraced it as personal to themselves. The song transports you into a reverie that is warm and welcoming and seems to enfold you in a timeless joy, even though any objective reading of the title reveals that it's a song about the very opposite of warmth and welcome and joy.

But I'm sure most of the Procol Harum fanbase would agree with me on this: something went horribly wrong when the band decided to start their career with the song. I don't want to denigrate 'Pale' or its success and influence (it deserves all its praise), but it wrecked the group before they'd even properly begun. There were other songs that could have been released first, delaying 'Pale' a month at most. 'Salad Days' was in the running for debut single, though it would have been better to choose 'Conquistador' or (ideally) 'Kaleidoscope' if that had been written in time. The band needed *something* to ground themselves as a unit. On eventual release, 'Pale' would have soared every bit as high, and there wouldn't have been all the turmoil at the top.

But still, before you rush to your time machine and go back to kick Brooker in the shin on his way to the studio in early 1967, we might easily have lost so much. We'd never have the classic lineup, perhaps – never have had Robin Trower and B.J. Wilson in the band. Hence, we'd never have had so much of what we now revere about the group. Any delay in the song's accidental but perfectly timed arrival in May 1967 may well have blunted its impact, given the roar of psychedelia that followed *Sgt. Pepper's Lonely Hearts Club Band* the same month and 'All You Need Is Love' in July. 'Pale' succeeded because it hit the airwaves just *before* The Beatles bounced back into the frame. Afterwards, well, how dated that first Procol Harum album seemed within months of 'Pale'. And without the immense success and instant millstone of the single, Brooker might never have reacted in the ways he did, pushing the band into the experiments of *Shine On Brightly* and beyond.

We might have had nothing at all if Brooker's recollection to *Newsweek* in July 1967 is true: 'We were all poor. We were borrowing bubble-and-squeak money from each other. The feeling was we would probably break up after this one record. If it made it, okay. If it didn't, goodbye'. That's borne out by the publicity footage that accompanied 'Pale', in which Brooker looked positively skeletal.

I certainly do wish that 'Kaleidoscope' had come *after* 'Pale' as the second single. 'Kaleidoscope' was different and catchy enough to have been a hit and would have altered critical perceptions of the group for the better. But in our reality, we're stuck with a golden crown that turned to thorns. 'Pale' made the band and then broke the band twice over. Firstly, when the *ad hoc* aggregation of musicians formed to promote it busted apart at the height of their British chart success, and again when the music papers refused to see the band as anything more than a moment in time that passed like a perfect summer romance, and which later seemed – in the way of such romances – as just a bit embarrassing to recall.

The origin of Reid's lyric has been well documented since everybody asked him about it. At some point in 1966, Reid and Brooker attended a party at Guy Stevens's house. His wife Diane (who dated the party to around June) turned pallid for some reason, and Stevens commented to her, 'You've turned a whiter shade of pale'. Reid overheard the remark, and the song composed itself as a series of woozy, hallucinogenic images: the party, the dancing, the girl, too much drink, and something or other that causes her to blanch in shock, fear, or embarrassment. Reid explained the songwriting process to *The Daily Express* in 1997: 'It's like making a pot. You get your initial idea – here I had that line 'a whiter shade of pale' – so you've got your bit of clay, and then you just try to make a pot out of it. And you use your imagination, you shape it and play with it until you've got something that looks like a pot or sounds like a song'.

In Reid's obituary in *Classic Rock* in 2023, Brooker explained how the results were delivered to him: 'Keith had written the lyrics and posted them to me. I'd been working on a musical idea which until then had been purely instrumental, when I opened the post and 'A Whiter Shade Of Pale' was on the top of other lyrics. I was immediately taken by the immense length of the original four verses, with a chorus on each, and the narrative form it took with its mysterious characters and goings-on'.

There were indeed originally four verses, but for the sake of radio airplay, these were soon cut to two. I'm not convinced they needed to be since Bob Dylan's 'Like A Rolling Stone' had originally been released in 1965 as a six-minute single (in both the UK and USA) with a three-minute promo version to deal with radio restrictions. Still, the nascent Procol Harum were taking no chances.

The only real mystery in the lyric is what caused Diane Stevens's change of face colour. She hasn't explained what afflicted her, and anyway, it's likely it was irrelevant to Reid's thought process. In the song, the reaction appears to be to a recitation of *The Miller's Tale* – Geoffrey Chaucer's infamously bawdy 14th-century poem of inadvertent ass-kissing and a red hot plough blade. But Reid told the *Huffington Post* in 2009: 'I knew who Chaucer was, but can't say I read him. It's not a quote in any way whatsoever. People said, 'You're very into *The Miller's Tale* by Chaucer', but I can't say I was that bookish'.

So *this* miller could be something quite different – a real or imagined man named Miller at the party or someone with the figurative function of a miller: for example, a manager, promoter, or DJ who grinds up prospective pop stars. There's no hidden key to the piece in the excised verses, at least one of which the band were performing in concert by the time of our first official live recording of the song in 1975, and both of which begin Reid's obsession with the sea. What's notable about both is that they have *exactly* the same kind of uncouth bawdiness as Chaucer's tale. In one, the woman is described savagely as 'the mermaid who took Neptune for a ride'. In the other, she and the narrator 'attacked the ocean bed'. Neither is a particularly sophisticated allusion, let alone the blatantly earthy sexual foreplay of lines like 'If behind is in front/Then dirt in truth is clean'. Shocking as it may seem to those who think the song to be an outpouring of chivalrous love, 'Pale' is actually just a whisker away from 'Luskus Delph', Reid's 1971 song, as a catalogue of references to female genitals.

From all this, you might presume that Reid himself is the miller whose vulgar ways caused the girl to blanch, except his advances were apparently successful. (The grinding, then, is exactly what you think it is.) 'Pale' demonstrated that songwriters could get away with vulgarity as long as it was literary enough that public gatekeepers such as the BBC and the Gavin Report didn't understand it. This was a lesson Procol Harum fan John Lennon failed to fully take to heart in his 'Pale'-style composition 'I Am The Walrus' later the same year, but which stood Jimmy Webb in great stead with 'MacArthur Park' the next year. 'Pressed in love's hot fevered iron like a striped pair of pants' is pure Reid obfuscation, while the dress 'foaming like a wave on the ground around your knees' shows exactly the same delight in mental gymnastics and ever-so-rude-if-you-look-at-it-askance surrealism.

With the lyric in Brooker's possession and propped on his piano, it's at this point that we have to tread *extremely* carefully regarding the composition of 'Pale' since the ground becomes strewn with legal broken glass. Certainly, we can say that Reid wrote the words and Brooker wrote some music that happened to match. But we have to align the tune with Brooker's admiration for French pianist Jacques Loussier, who'd been recording light-jazz versions of Bach pieces since 1959. Loussier's 1966 single 'Air On A G String' is most familiar to British listeners from TV advertisements for Hamlet cigars. Brooker told *The Daily Express* in 1997 that this was the origin of his music: 'I was living in Southend at the time, with my Mum. I had been fascinated by a piece of music that was on the TV a lot in the Hamlet cigar adverts. They only used the Jacques Loussier recording. I knew the piece anyway in the back of my mind, but it came to prominence with the Hamlet ads, and that was about the beginning of '67, I think'.

The least we can say is that Brooker acknowledged the debt and that the verses of 'Pale' are a variation on the same basic chords. The soaring chorus is something else again. Brooker's model for that might have been Percy Sledge's 1966 hit 'When A Man Loves A Woman', though Brooker denied it.

And that's as much as we can say. Having used the first *Melody Maker* advert to hire the basic shape of the band, and with studio sessions booked for March, Procol Harum still needed the all-important organist. This time, the player presented himself to *them*. Organist Matthew Fisher used the *Melody Maker* listings to hire himself out to touring bands since just *owning* a Hammond made him hot property. That he was an immensely proficient player educated at Guildhall School of Music made pop seem like easy work.

We can date Fisher's initial involvement with the band precisely to the 25 February *Melody Maker* advert that caught Brooker's eye: 'Hammond organist, harmony vocals, seeks pro. group', followed by a Croydon number. They were lucky. Fisher was competent and amenable, and they hired him on the spot. His first great contribution to the band was to devise the trademark organ flourish that makes 'Pale' instantly irresistible.

It's a shame there are no surviving demos showing what the song sounded like before his arrival. Then we could properly parse assertions such as the following, made to *SongwriterUniverse* in 2020, about the day Brooker received Reid's words: 'I sang them over my idea, and that became the tune, along with the instrumental passages I played in between'. Or this, which Brooker made to *Rolling Stone* in 1971: 'We got a few musicians together and hired a demo studio. One of the songs we cut was 'A Whiter Shade Of Pale'. It was exactly like the single that was released later, except less well-recorded, naturally'.

With no other evidence to hand, we must accept Fisher's word that what he added was deserving of a writing credit, though he had to take Brooker to court in 2005 to receive it. It also seems astonishing today that neither Brooker nor anybody else associated with the band realised just what a phenomenal piece of work they had created *until* Fisher added his organ.

What at first was merely the joy of being associated with a hit group soon rankled the organist. Fisher complained to *Uncut* magazine in 2008:

It was entirely my idea to compose a set solo and to give the last two bars a satisfying shape. What I added was a tune, of course. I saw a proof of the sheet music, and the first thing I saw was that the first eight bars were my organ solo. And yet, at the top of the sheet music, it said: 'Music by Gary

Brooker'. Suddenly, I realised what I had contributed went way beyond
the call of duty. Gary was totally unsympathetic, and I was completely
devastated.

Had the wound been mortal, you might have expected action sooner. Instead,
Fisher was an integral part of the band until 1969, rejoined it in 1991, and
remained a performing member for another 14 years until his lawsuit. He only
began to assert his composition of the motif in 1973. The case came down to
him claiming the organ parts as his own work and Brooker offering scant proof
to refute him. The result was controversial but inevitable. Since 2005, Fisher has
been awarded a retrospective writing credit and his due share of the royalties.

And let's celebrate his win. Fisher's organ-playing capped the song, gave it
a hook and a contrast to Brooker's meandering verses, and made it special.
In common with almost all early Procol Harum songs, 'Pale' lacks a middle
eight. Instead, Fisher plays his composition twice, and provides a variation
at the end: the closest the piece comes to a solo or an improvisation. Even
this variation goes through what seems to be structured changes, giving the
impression of a fully composed piece summoned from the depths of time: the
primal music of the church of the soul.

It was a scarcely prepared band of novices that rushed into Olympic Studio
on 29 March to record it. They still lacked a proper drummer, choosing session
player Bill Eyden to keep the beat. There were three hurried takes without
overdubs. Fisher's Hammond is the hook, while the rest of the instruments are
a disorientating rush of time-dilating reverb, particularly on Eyden's cymbals,
giving the song the feel that you're listening to it from somewhere far off
down the other end of the nave of a great cathedral. But none of its positives
(not Fisher's magnificent playing, not Reid's mesmerising words) would have
counted for anything had it not been for Brooker's serenely regal vocal: a very
real, very relatable human connection in the vaults of the night.

The released mono single was the third take. The second take was first issued
on Westside's *30th Anniversary Anthology* in 1997, also in mono. It runs for
5:45, ends with a breakdown rather than a fade, and lacks vocals except for a
guide deep in the mix, enabling you to fully savour Fisher's inventive playing
– that is, if you can restrain yourself from the near-irresistible pull of karaoke.
Like the single, there's no discernible Ray Royer guitar, but Brooker's piano is
more prominent. The extended ending circles around and around the chorus.
Let's assume the first take was a bust since it has never surfaced.

After the session, neither the band nor their management were convinced
by what they'd achieved. They even considered it for the B-side to 'Salad
Days' or a song called 'Alpha' (the tale of a Cyclops child abandoned by his
parents in a church, who finds employment, if not peace, as a bell-ringing
Quasimodo) or one of the other compositions they had ready. Nor was there
much of an industry response. Even Decca's 'progressive' subsidiary Deram
(home to hits by Cat Stevens and The Move) rejected the piece.

Concerned by the sound defects in the recording – in particular Eyden's thrashing cymbals – in mid-April, Cordell snuck an acetate to pirate radio station Radio London (this was just ahead of the formation of BBC Radio One) to gauge how it sounded on the air. Meanwhile, on 19 April, he took the band to Advision Studios (as its name suggests, primarily an advertising-jingle studio) to record another version, this time utilising the band's new drummer, Bobby Harrison. In the event, the Radio London broadcast proved that the original 'Pale' was acceptable. The Advision version was filed away, but that session did provide the B-side.

The band have never released a stereo 'Pale' from Olympic. However, there *is* a stereo 'Pale' from the Advision session, also issued on the *30th Anniversary Anthology*. Introduced as 'take two', it runs to 5:51, again has nothing resembling a guitar, comes to an ill-advised conclusion, and suffers from Harrison's unstable drumming, which seems to drag the entire band into a listless, exhausted reading that hobbles even this most lethargic of tempos. Regardless, Brooker's vocal is so good that it breaks your heart all over again every time you play it.

The audience response to the Radio London broadcast – instant and phenomenal – convinced Deram to give the song another listen, and the single was released on 12 May, just three weeks after its recording. 'Pale' rocketed up the British charts and surely would have lodged at number one for more than its six weeks had 'All You Need Is Love' (the first Beatles single in four months and launched with an immense TV fanfare) not finally given it a shove back downstairs. The classical music critic for *The Times*, William Mann, who had championed Lennon and McCartney in 1964 as modern classical composers, now saw 'Pale' as part of an even greater sophistication in pop. On 29 May, he wrote: 'There is the rare but often appealing grope back to classical or baroque musical language, as in the Alberti string figuration of The Beatles' 'Eleanor Rigby' and the new, distinctly Bach-derived 'Whiter Shade Of Pale' by the Procol Harum, which has its pop parentage in some Animals numbers, and is very beautiful indeed'.

The achievement was even greater in the US, which that June had seemed to look across at the single's success in England and the rest of Europe as if there was a vast tidal wave forming on the eastern horizon. America merely waited for it to deluge the country. When it did, 'Pale' ascended the charts without the hope of a promotional appearance on the continent, sold in the millions, and made the band's name for perpetuity. Ironically, while all this was happening, Procol Harum had busted apart and had, to all intents and purposes, blown it as an act.

'Lime Street Blues' (Brooker, Reid)
Those purchasers who bothered to check out the B-side were to find a legend-deflating mundanity, a song every bit as ordinary as its A-side was extraordinary. 'Lime Street Blues' is a huge-selling obscurity, a song largely

overlooked even in Procol Harum compilations. It's a piano-driven R&B rave-up, indistinguishable from the early singles by The Paramounts save for one startling differentiator: a Reid lyric that is simultaneously as comically outré as Bob Dylan or Frank Zappa and so poorly written that it's either juvenile or a gauche parody of itself.

It begins, 'Lime Street in the afternoon/Everybody crazy as a coon'. The Americanism is as distancing as 'We tripped the light fandango' was enveloping. Reid spins the rueful first-person tale of a hooker with bleached blonde 'golden locks' who is arrested and pleads for mercy in court as a 'poor orphan child'. It doesn't save her. In principle, rewriting the Liverpudlian folk song 'Maggie Mae' (raucously recorded by The Beatles in 1969) as a transatlantic outlaw tale from the prostitute's point of view was a good idea, but Reid wasn't yet up to the task and this has nothing of the power or sympathy of Bob Dylan's own courtroom piece 'Percy's Song'.

It's a throwaway for sure, but not completely valueless. The band played well (something of a surprise given the way Procol Harum devotees have been taught to think about Royer and Harrison) and there's some lively organ chatter from Fisher. But the fast tempo and bluesy swing were a dead end for the band, a pandering to youthful energy that they ditched almost immediately in favour of something more measured and mature.

A Whiter Shade Of Pale (LP) (1967)

Details for tracks not previously released on the single:
Personnel:
Gary Brooker: piano, celeste, vocals
Matthew Fisher: organ
David Knights: bass
Robin Trower: guitar
B.J. Wilson: drums
Recorded: March-June 1967, Olympic Studios, London, UK
Producer: Denny Cordell
Label: Deram (US), Regal Zonophone (UK)
Release date: September 1967 (US), December 1967 (UK)
Charts: US: 47
Running time (US): 37:21 (A: 18:09, B: 19:12)
Running time (UK): 34:22 (A: 16:37, B: 17:45)
Tracklisting in North America: 'A Whiter Shade Of Pale', 'She Wandered Through The Garden Fence', 'Something Following Me', 'Mabel', 'Cerdes (Outside The Gates Of)', 'A Christmas Camel', 'Conquistador', 'Kaleidoscope/Salad Days (Are Here Again)', 'Repent Walpurgis'
Tracklisting in UK: 'Conquistador', 'She Wandered Through The Garden Fence', 'Something Following Me', 'Mabel', 'Cerdes (Outside The Gates Of)', 'A Christmas Camel', 'Kaleidoscope', 'Salad Days (Are Here Again)', 'Good Captain Clack', 'Repent Walpurgis'
Tracklisting in most other territories: 'Homburg', 'She Wandered Through The Garden Fence', 'Something Following Me', 'Mabel', 'Cerdes (Outside The Gates Of)', 'A Christmas Camel', 'Kaleidoscope', 'Salad Days (Are Here Again)', 'Conquistador', 'Repent Walpurgis'

The covers of *Melody Maker* in June and July 1967 tell a fascinating story. At the beginning of May, nobody had heard of Procol Harum. In the edition dated 27 May, the band gained the small three-paragraph article 'Procol Harum single roars into chart' on an inside page, dwarfed by a headline about The Monkees gaining a second series on the BBC. It noted that Procol Harum were about to appear on *Top Of The Pops* and were to make their concert debut at the Saville Theatre on 4 June alongside The Jimi Hendrix Experience and ex-Moody Blues singer Denny Laine's Electric String Band.

On 10 June, the cover was dominated by a close-up photo of Gary Brooker in a Chinese cap. 'Harum scarum right to top!' blared the article, which breathlessly listed the band's achievements in its three months of existence. Then, on 15 July, there was another front-page photo, this time of all five group members looking sour-faced in a London street. 'Procol split up – two quit!' shrieked the above-the-fold block capitals.

The very idea of it seems absurd. The band blazed to the top of the charts, stayed there for weeks, and while they were still the hottest and most feted band in Britain (and arguably all the parts of the world that had heard the single by then), fizzled out like those fireworks that whizz up promisingly only to puff out a few coloured balls and expire.

It was likely the 15 July headline (more even than the unrepeatable time capsule of the single) that soured the press on the band and sealed their fate. Procol Harum were hardly alone in collapsing under the strain of the 1967 pop grind (the same thing happened to 'See Emily Play' hit-makers The Pink Floyd at exactly the same time) and hardly alone too in turning the stress inward, picking out the weaker members to blame. Nor did it help that the press thought the band had been manufactured to ride the 'Pale' promotion machine or that when guitarist Ray Royer and drummer Bobby Harrison were booted out (neither of whom were actually on the single), Brooker drafted in two of his old Paramounts colleagues: Robin Trower (seemingly now eager to join) and B. J. Wilson. It also didn't help that lawsuits started flying around, including one from that cymbal-happy session player Bill Eyden, nor that the whole mess was incompetently covered up with the same claims of mental and physical exhaustion that The Pink Floyd had used to hide their own troubles.

At the very peak of Procol Harum's fame, Royer, Harrison, and the band's management team were all jettisoned, and all the sessions recorded over the same period were scratched. There was an album waiting to press – every song that was eventually released on the UK version of the band's debut had already been recorded at Olympic in May and June, with the sole exception of 'Good Captain Clack', a later song first employed as the B-side to the second single 'Homburg'. There was even a Royer/Harrison version of 'Repent Walpurgis'.

The new lineup with Trower and Wilson recorded the whole thing over in a handful of hurried sessions in July.

Brooker unloaded on the whole sorry mess to *The Daily Express* in 1997, putting the blame firmly on Royer and Harrison: 'When we got into the studio seriously with the drummer and guitarist, their style didn't really fit. We tried seven or eight songs, then Denny Cordell said, 'Look, this is not working out', and I said, 'No', and he said, 'We'll have to find another drummer and guitarist'. It all turned bad, horribly bad. I don't think people have ever got over that in Britain'.

It may well be more complicated than this. The concert debut at the Saville Theatre was a disaster. The papers savaged the performance, complaining that the band were boring and lacked any kind of stage appeal and that all their songs were the same plodding dirge. Denny Cordell rushed to try to salvage their live reputation, but you can't come back from a collective groan of disappointment. Cordell told *Melody Maker* on 17 June: 'Their music is stimulating intellectually as well as emotionally. It's pretty introverted music and definitely not for leaping about. They are mood makers and should be listened to whilst stoned out of your mind at 3 a.m'.

Reid, not helping matters much, scoffed to the *New Musical Express*: 'We are as we are. It is the public's prerogative to accept or reject us. We don't make a conscious attempt to be ourselves or anything else'.

All that aside, this chapter is complicated by the fact that the Trower/Wilson album was released in three separate versions in different territories. There was also an exception in Italy, notable for its bright purple cover, which had unique versions of 'Homburg' and the Italian single 'Il Tuo Diamente' (for which see the *Shine On Brightly* chapter), and gave 'Repent Walpurgis' the name 'Fortuna', which seemingly justified a writing credit for the Italian lyricist Dossena. Yet another version of the album was issued in 1972, and the work has been reissued many times since with all kinds of listings and a jumble of bonus tracks.

Because the band were British, it's normal to consider the UK edition as definitive. However, the North American edition was released significantly earlier (as was the case with all early Procol Harum albums) and sold in quantities large enough to chart there, so it surely has the greater claim. More people owned it and they owned it first. Though the presentations were near-identical (a cover drawing by Reid's future wife 'Dickinson' who also provided the covers for *A Salty Dog* and *Home)*, the titles (*A Whiter Shade Of Pale* in North America, *Procol Harum* in the UK) and contents were different. The rest of this chapter lists the album-exclusive tracks in North American order.

Of all the bad management decisions that hamstrung Procol Harum in their home country, the choice to delay release of the album until the end of the year – too late even for the Christmas market – meant it was doomed by the time it finally trickled out to an audience that had long since passed its high psychedelic phase and was now forging ahead into Vanilla Fudge-style progressive rock. A one-dimensional album in Dylan's old style, resolutely recorded in mono by stereo-averse producer Denny Cordell, and which didn't even have the decency to include the hits (due to licensing restrictions with the new label Regal Zonophone), stood no chance at the turn into 1968. 'To be listened to in the spirit in which it was made', stated the sour back cover quote, essentially an excuse for inflicting something so ramshackle on the public.

Having blown it *again*, the album saw the beginning of the systematic lack of press regard for Procol Harum in the UK that meant they would be afforded little praise there no matter how fine they became as a recording and live act – and Procol Harum soon became very fine indeed. Still, many fans rate the album highly, with or without *that single* sitting at the top of it. The band themselves have expressed ambivalent views. To *Creem*, Reid gushed in 1972: 'It was fantastic, you know. I thought all the songs were great. It was the worst-recorded album, but I really like it. I like the excitement of it. It was great, a great feeling, a great time making it'. In *Hit Parader* the same year, specifically referencing Cordell's production, Reid called the album 'totally diabolical'.

Robin Trower said much the same. He told *Zigzag* in 1972: 'I think the material on that album is the best Procol ever had. It was just bad luck that we didn't have the right producer or manager. If we'd had someone to spend a lot of time and record that material with the imagination and love it deserved, then that probably would have been one of the classic albums of all time'.

Brooker was candid about the real reasons for the disc's failure. Procol Harum had already wasted a run of expensive sessions recording the Royer/Harrison version, and what revenue the single was bringing in was used fighting legal cases against ex-members and ex-management. He told *New Musical Express* in 1971: 'We didn't have the time or the money. It was the second time that we'd made that album. We made it once and we then scrapped it and made it again. We made it in three days. It was very rushed. We were doing six songs in one evening, which was too much'.

As for the critics, the ones that reviewed the North American issue (when the sound was still fresh enough to be interesting) were generally positive. Of special note was Paul Williams, whose lengthy *Crawdaddy* piece in September 1967 begat a whole new set of troubles to come when he began to trace Procol Harum (rather than Bob Dylan's contemporaneous but then largely unknown *Basement Tapes*) as the missing link between Dylan's *Blonde On Blonde* and The Band's *Music From Big Pink*. Of 'Cerdes' he wrote: 'More and more you feel the want of the music to devour the vocalist. When he returns after the break, he is inside, lost, swallowed. This is the approach to the void, a newer 'Gates Of Eden' – a comparison of the songs will show you how far we've gone, in only two years, how much closer we are, how much less we know'.

In the band's *annus mirabilis* 1972, the UK version of the album was reissued there as a double paired with *A Salty Dog*. This time, the hit single was added to the start of side one, and the album was titled *A Whiter Shade Of Pale*. The set reached 26, meaning that technically, it *has* charted in the UK since we can be sure *A Salty Dog* didn't cause all the excitement. ('Pale' was also reissued as a single that year, reaching 13 in the UK.) It's this hybrid version that became standard in all territories, at least until CDs confused things again.

Though the album was recorded in mono, the North American version was artificially processed into stereo. True stereo versions of 'Conquistador', 'She Wandered Through The Garden Fence', and 'Homburg' were created in 1971 for the compilation *Flyback 4 – The Best Of Procol Harum*. True stereo versions of a couple of other tracks are available on albums such as *Pandora's Box* (1999). There's no true stereo version of the entire Trower/Wilson album as originally released.

'She Wandered Through The Garden Fence' (Brooker, Reid)
The first new song on the North American album repeats the Procol Harum trait of quoting from other people's work: the very basis of the classical feel

of 'A Whiter Shade Of Pale'. There was never any subterfuge. Brooker and Fisher were happy to tell interviewers which pieces they'd incorporated into their own tune. Brooker revealed that when stuck for a melody, he would place Bach sheet music on his piano and play it until he found a sequence he liked and then build a song around those notes. Hence, it's likely there are a lot *more* Bach quotes in Procol Harum than we know.

In this case, there's a clear lift from Jeremiah Clarke's *Prince Of Denmark's March* (better known as a 'trumpet voluntary') in Fisher's organ solos at 1:33 and 2:59. Trainspotting Procol Harum quotes is something of a fan sport but is largely incidental to the band's appeal. The band weren't the first to use such devices, but the habit was to become endemic among prog-rock bands in their wake. Yes's early albums repeat Procol Harum's mix of highbrow and lowbrow steals: a Holst reference one moment, the theme from *The Big Country* the next.

Its historical importance aside, 'She Wandered Through The Garden Fence' is also notable for the disconnect between music and lyric that was to become another of the band's traits. The song is upbeat, chirpy, a vehicle for Fisher's garrulous organ-playing, like a gaggle of housewives gossiping at their washing lines. Reid's words are dour, sullen, a doctor's waiting room of complaints. The only way these two incompatible elements could possibly be reconciled (the glue that holds so many Procol Harum songs together) was with the soulful sincerity of Brooker's voice, which both deepens the pop and leavens the despair.

Reid's lyric here is weird even by 'Pale' standards. The song relates the narrator's disastrous encounter with an imaginary *femme fatale* – probably a manifestation of his own guilt – who punishes him physically for his sins. He's eventually released, chastened, wiser, and less ashamed of himself. A religious corrective, then, of the basest sort and a theme that was to be repeated in songs to come. Of note is the touch of wordplay that – like many of Reid's puns – strays dangerously close to a schoolboy smirk. Having been strapped on a rack, the narrator finds his mind 'was also bent/Upon a course so devious'. It's fun redirection, but like later, more-lauded examples (in particular the 'Homburg' phrase 'the mirror, on reflection'), it's not really much more than a surface cleverness.

'Something Following Me' (Brooker, Reid)
This is solemn, heartfelt blues – a style which means blues devotee Robin Trower is able to plug in, though, for most of the song, all he contributes are growls deep in the mix. The rolling rock arrangement, with Fisher's washes adding depth (rather than the busyness of 'She Wandered Through The Garden Fence'), is the album's first overt link back to the piano-based work on Bob Dylan's *Highway 61 Revisited*. An even stronger link will follow. When Trower steps forward, his solo is truly startling: an abrupt blaze of fuzz that is far too fierce for the song, reducing everything else to monochrome-like eyes that have yet to adjust to sunlight.

The lyric – which apparently first attracted Brooker to Reid – is compelling, though the phrasing is a little unsophisticated and Reid leans too heavily on Dylan's talking-blues style of quasi-mythical first-person reportage. However, America called to Reid, even this early: the song takes place in New York. A man is pursued around the city by the tombstone that represents his own mortality, even though he 'thought I'd left it at home': death as the second secret shame in a row.

'Mabel' (Brooker, Reid)

After all that gloom, 'Mabel' is a pause for breath before the darkness closes in for good, and as such, it's utterly misplaced in the album sequence. It might have been a better opener for side two or even relegated to a single B-side where it could function as an optional novelty. The song's a brief cockney sing-along in the style Small Faces turned into a career, with uncredited guests joining in on percussion, slide whistle, clinking coins, and violin, and a rabble of whooping drunks shouting the words from the bar. But again, it's awkwardly transatlantic due to a good-time jug band sound that Reid claimed was based on The Lovin' Spoonful; hence, this is a joint somewhere in downtown New York.

Though also uncredited, the basic track is a holdover from the Royer/ Harrison sessions; hence, it's Harrison who drums rather than Wilson. There's no sign of guitar to give Ray Royer a claim on the album.

It's the first of Reid's food songs. But unlike 'Fresh Fruit' on *Exotic Birds And Fruit*, there's no overt innuendo in the singer's exhortations to his girl to stop dancing on the table and get on with the cooking. More pleasing is the *real* sexual reference in 'Banish inhibition with a pogo stick', plus the intimation that the reason for all this carousing is that the singer's wife is lying stabbed in the cellar. There's also the use of an image that was brewing in 'Homburg' (a song recorded at the same time) and was to surface fully in the surrealism of 'Shine On Brightly': 'Your sundial's wrong'.

'Cerdes (Outside The Gates Of)' (Brooker, Reid)

The album's centrepiece – Brooker and Reid's second great triumph after 'Pale', and the best composition of the band's first year – is the longest song on the album (5:00), beaten in length only by the instrumental 'Repent Walpurgis' which is slightly under a second longer, and the longest self-contained Procol Harum song until 'Whaling Stories' in 1970. It's compelling and houses what has a strong claim to being Reid's best lyric.

The title reveals the song to be a homage to Dylan's 'Gates Of Eden', but it's more than this. The reference enables Reid to accrue all of Dylan's values onto himself, as if 'Cerdes' is a diffraction from the same jewel of thought. This means that what on first reading may seem to be a tumble of disconnected phrases demands analysis as both a surrealist train of associations and as poetry. In effect, just as 'Pale' borrowed its gravitas from Bach, so 'Cerdes' borrowed its gravitas from Dylan.

The title is the first of Reid's references to an inscrutable mental logic: a word like those of 'Luskus Delph' that seems familiar even if it's invented, and that is steeped in associations all its own, just as Pink Floyd were to do with their similarly icy 'Cirrus Minor' two years later. Like that song, this is an emissary from deep space (the name is reminiscent of the asteroid Ceres), and it also links with childhood readings of Greek and Roman mythology. The effect is glimpsed, shadowy, and threatening. Whatever this realm is, it's every bit as dangerous as Dylan's godless wilderness and as bleak as his Desolation Row.

Populating the landscape are freaks and failures, each frozen in time like the chiselled stone relief of an infernal carnival. We meet a caricature of Elvis Presley: a 'two-pronged unicorn' playing 'a rhinestone flugelhorn'. We meet the mermaids and Neptune of 'Pale' again, this time grimacing in their watery prisons. There's a Biblical reference, though it's to Salome dancing at a beheading rather than the Old Testament horrors with which Dylan crowded his deeps. The juxtaposition of Neptune's hornpipe (a sailor's dance to amuse his fellows) and Salome's dance (a striptease to arouse strangers) is truly horrifying. Both are trapped – like Reid, like Brooker, arguably like all pop entertainers – in the gurning squalor of their need to please others.

Deeper in, we reach the pit of fictional characters: Phallus Phil, Sousa Sam, Peep The Sot, artists whose creations are deformed and drunken poets whose verse has curdled in their mouths. And in the final verse, science itself has distorted into 'wraiths' and 'greeps' whose falsehoods are now indistinguishable from truth. It's all a marvellous atrocity, palatable only if you don't quite catch what Reid is saying, and a very good reason why he long resisted the call to include a lyric sheet in Procol Harum albums.

Just as 'She Wandered Through The Garden Gate' built itself around Wilson's drumming, so 'Cerdes' accumulates over David Knights's simple but mesmerising bass riff – bluesy enough for Trower to find his place, and with the monolithic propulsion and lumbering-forward of a vast indefatigable machine that we would later associate with heavy metal. It's the moment the band found their feet, the true base of their sound (sidelining 'Pale' as a poppy aberration), and a style that would be perfected over the following four albums until *Broken Barricades* – on the cusp of Trower's departure – brought the band fully to grips with its power. The guitar solo is extended, emphatic, and of a masterful ability that Trower would later match but never exceed. Consumed in the majesty of the piece, all Fisher can do is stomp his elbows on his Hammond keys, defining at a stroke everything that Jon Lord brought to Deep Purple.

'A Christmas Camel' (Brooker, Reid)

Flipping the LP gave original listeners the chance to recover from the onslaught of 'Cerdes' and refresh their ears for side two. That's not the case on CD, where 'A Christmas Camel' follows on immediately and comes across as an inevitable lag in energy and invention. The silly title doesn't help. Charitably, the pun on 'carol' is meant to represent Camel cigarettes and, by association, the cigars that husbands allowed themselves as their Christmas indulgence, or – far less likely – a sneaky nod to cannabis. Less charitably, it's a reminder that the Holy Land is in the desert and is the first of Reid's recurring and sometimes derogatory references to Arabs.

While you can build a credible case for Reid the poet in 'Cerdes', I'm not convinced the same is possible here. The intention is identical: a host of vivid but disconnected images bouncing past one after the other, some of which the listener may be able to unpick objectively, some of which make sense only from Reid's perspective, and some of which likely have no meaning whatsoever. We may seem to glimpse Reid in these words due to recurring mannerisms – there appears to be another intimation of 'Homburg' in the lines 'I am overcome with shame/And hide inside my overcoat' – but we can't be sure. My suspicion is that 'A Christmas Camel' is ear candy to go with its yuletide references: glittery, colourful, fattening, but empty.

Musically, it's based on the same block-chord piano blues as Dylan's 'Ballad Of A Thin Man', which may be another clue to the title since Dylan describes Mr. Jones as walking into the room 'like a camel'. Fisher obliges with an Al Kooper impersonation, and he's figured out what Kooper understood and Lord would understand after him – that if he let the rest of the band lay down the song structure, he could whirl all over the top of it and be essentially the only member free to have fun in the moment. But again, it's Trower who gets the feature, and again, his fierce, carefully scripted phrases are the crown of the song.

'Conquistador' (Brooker, Reid)

In the album's North American version, we now get two strong up-tempo songs in a row, colliding them awkwardly. Though for a while 'Conquistador' was in the running as the second US single, it wasn't released there at the time. But the band evidently thought enough of the song to make it the lead cut on the UK album. It did manage a single release in Australia, where it almost made the charts.

Retrospectively, this is one of the few times Reid was *aware* that Brooker's tune came first. He told *Songfacts* in 2009:

We had this regular deal where he lived about 40 miles from London near the ocean, and I'd jump on a train once a week and go visit him. He'd have a bunch of my lyrics and he'd play me whatever he had been working on. This particular time, though, I'd got down there and he'd been working on a tune. He said, 'What does this sound like to you?' and I said, 'Oh, conquistador'. It had a little bit of a Spanish flavour to it. I went into another room and started writing the words there and then.

The result was another triumph and an indication that the two men could create magic on demand. The remarkable thing about 'Conquistador' as it stood at the head of the UK album is that it was resolutely not a song about love but death, and though more references to death follow, there isn't one love song on the entire album. Thanks to 'Lovely Rita', The Beatles couldn't even make that claim about *Sgt. Pepper*. Reid's concise verses describe the corpse of a fallen warrior left on a foreign beach; his vanity turned to tarnished armour and carrion. For the moment, only his horse remains faithful. But soon, others will come to plunder his jewels in the same way he came to plunder the Americas. The singer mourns his death but finds no lesson in it.

The music that inspired this keen poetry is notable not so much for its Spanish flavour as for the restraint that Brooker brought to the original arrangement: the opposite of the florid Mexicana that propelled a live recording of the song into a hit in 1972. Its allusions are subtle and culturally vague, making 'Conquistador' actually a song of universal hubris. Like Ozymandias, the mighty tumble and are forgotten. There's the same sympathy in Brooker's treatment of the words as, say, for a deceased nobody in 'Nothing That I Didn't Know' on *Home*: a life is lost, regardless of its grandeur or humility. With no change whatsoever, you can imagine 'Conquistador' slotting in perfectly on the latter album, teetering like much of *Home* between mournful introspection and hard-nosed rock spitting angry volume over yet another grave.

'Kaleidoscope' (Brooker, Reid)
In their first year as songwriting partners, Brooker and Reid amassed a war chest of pieces that populated not only the first album and two hit singles but part of what became *Shine On Brightly* and a number of offcuts to which the band returned in later years. With all this material to draw on, it's perplexing that they concentrated on throwaways like 'Lime Street Blues' and 'Alpha' when a composition as strong and commercial as 'Kaleidoscope' was already in the running. The only way the song slipped through the cracks is if it were a late addition to the roster from a time when 'Homburg' was in progress: after the chaos of June, say.

Instead, the song was consigned to the relative obscurity of side two and, in the North American edition, wasn't even afforded the dignity of being listed as a separate track. That release grouped this and 'Salad Days' as a single piece running 6:31. Both tracks may have been originally written for movies. The rear cover noted that 'Salad Days' was featured in *Separation* (1968), then in production. *Separation* also featured some solo instrumental work by Fisher. The cover didn't note that Reid had submitted lyrics in early 1966 for the movie *Kaleidoscope* that were not used in that film. He certainly didn't submit music, at least not *Brooker's* music, but may well have exhumed the words for his new partner. Could Reid really have

31

been scratching around at this point to see what other lyrics he could give Brooker to fill out the album?

They're certainly arresting words and nothing like anything else the band were working up at the time. The frantic sentence fragments and disconnected shards of imagery describe the scurrying of pop and fashion that is now synonymous with the mirror dresses and slashing primaries of 1966 rather than the lazy paisley introspection of 1967. And this *is* surely London since it also has nothing in common with Dylan's beat verse.

If the song isn't better regarded, it's simply because it also displays evidence of the studio rush that followed the abandonment of the Royer/Harrison sessions. A little polish would have made it irresistible to radio – for example, something added to enliven the underdeveloped organ chord sequences that follow the chorus or a better Trower solo. Just think what Joe Boyd could have done with the piece over at Sound Techniques.

So, we lost the song in 1967. It's no compensation, but the exuberance with which the band resurrected 'Kaleidoscope' live four decades later at least gave it the respect it always deserved. But in better hands, well, what a treasure we might have had.

'Salad Days (Are Here Again)' (Brooker, Reid)

We've met this song already, as a reject from the 'Pale' single session. Nestled instead into the album, it forms a moment of introspection between the exuberance of 'Kaleidoscope' and the all-out prog-rock assault of 'Repent Walpurgis'. In isolation, it's not that much of a piece, but the understated confessional lyric may mark it as the first of Reid's autobiographical songs, assuming it's not merely a description of something he read in the script for *Separation*. There are correspondences with 'Homburg' and 'Shine On Brightly' – for example, the line 'For some unknown reason my watch begins to chime'. We're in the rumpled bed of what appears to be another broken relationship, though it's hard to tell if there was ever romance involved or if the singer is male or female.

Like the movie, it's a study in encroaching paranoia, with images that are either intimidating ('Your skin crawls up an octave') or transfixed, like LSD, on minutiae. Reid's most arresting line – 'The peaches snuggle closer down into the clotted cream' – is hilariously irrelevant (and it's another food reference!), and once you start to slither into its disagreeable imagery, it's sexually repugnant. The remnants of this affair are cold, slimy, and beginning to smell. Still, Reid's character puts on a public face, as signalled by the purposefully contrary title, a mix of Shakespeare's reference to the exuberance of youth and the jolly grin of the British movie *Happy Days Are Here Again*.

To leaven all this gloom, Brooker sets the words to a stately Dylan blues, with some of his most adept piano and a sheen of churchy depth from Fisher's organ, which takes the solo. There's no sign of Trower.

'Repent Walpurgis' (Fisher)

Despite all its other innovations, the most extraordinary thing about the album is this instrumental that rounds out side two. 'Repent Walpurgis' was as much a pinnacle for early Procol Harum as 'Pale' was. Both are rock refractions of classical music and features for Matthew Fisher's organ playing. At the same moment that The Beatles were erupting avant-garde orchestral music into pop on 'A Day In The Life', Fisher was laying down a template for the entire future of progressive rock as we would know it: amplified pomp played with great dexterity and utter conviction. There's no earlier evidence – not even from The Beatles themselves in their dalliances with establishment music – of just how thrilling an experience it is to hear powerful themes at ear-splitting volume.

There are plenty of highbrow and lowbrow steals in 'Repent Walpurgis' if you're inclined to winkle them out. Brooker said he took parts of the piece from different works by Bach. Fisher admitted that the bass line was lifted from the February 1967 Four Seasons single 'Beggin''. Though the piece is credited solely to Fisher, it's clear that it's a collaboration, and Brooker likely gave Fisher the credit as a nod to his work on 'Pale' and elsewhere. The structure itself seems to have been crafted by Brooker, in particular, the decision to interrupt the onslaught with a moment of calm. He told classicrockpage.com in 2000: 'I actually stuck the middle in it. I remember that because I thought it just went 'round and 'round and 'round, and I said: 'Well, let's add something different in the middle, Matthew. We'll just put this little part in'. And Matthew always wanted to call it 'Repent', and I thought it should be called 'Walpurgis', so we compromised'.

The piece's strength as a live workout was immediately obvious to the group. Brooker told *Crawdaddy* in 1970: 'We first played 'Repent Walpurgis' in the basement of a church. It went on for four or five hours without stopping. It was quite intense, really, almost unbearable'. By 'we', I assume he means the Trower/Wilson lineup since it's hard to think of the piece achieving anything like its impact with Royer on guitar and Harrison thrashing away on drums. No Royer/Harrison version has yet surfaced.

Like 'She Wandered Through The Garden Gate', the track begins with Wilson's rock-steady drumming, over which the band lays down what is essentially a reprise of the 'Pale' style, and at much the same tempo. A series of significant piano chords are played with arch solemnity, above which Fisher raises fists of organ holler. At 1:17, Trower enters for the first of his solos, a full minute in length. Brooker's soft-spoken piano arpeggios are sly misdirection, presenting the piece as acceptable to snoots in bowties: Trower's second entrance (at 3:27) tears the establishment down on their heads. It's a stunning scripted solo, every bit as fine as David Gilmour's more-lauded work, of which it is the clear forerunner. Even with the album's indifferent production and the limitations of mono to the modern listener, the triumphal ending leaves your ears blistered. It's a template for sure, but prog was to add nothing significantly new to what was already achieved here, just ever greater ways to achieve the same pulverising high.

When Brooker noted that the band would go ''round and 'round and 'round' playing 'Repent Walpurgis' for hours on end, we actually have studio evidence of it. The highlight of the 1999 rarities compilation *Pandora's Box* is a version of the piece that reprises its second half (from Brooker's piano arpeggios to the end) to bring the running time up to a monumental 7:24. It's in stereo, dated to August 1967, and not a performance from which the LP version was edited down. For a start, the band plays it faster, and there are also subtle arrangement differences, such as Trower's guitar stabs during the organ intro. He gears up into his first solo at 1:11, and, if anything, it's even better than the album take. Brooker begins his piano piece at 2:07, and again, a hopped-up Trower can't help stabbing along, though he wisely allows Fisher's anthemic chords to carry much of the first run-through of the finale, shouldering in only at 3:43 like he's in a hurry to get his fingers back on the frets. The band repeat the arpeggios section at 4:35, and this time, when they climb into the chords at 5:15, there's a palpable sense of a band grinning at the ferocity of their invention. Trower solos from the start, abetted by Wilson's fills. Somebody even whistles in joy at 6:29, just before the lengthy (and not altogether disciplined) collapse.

What this take might have done for the band's fortunes and for the rise of prog rock had the track been allowed to dominate the album is up for debate, but this is certainly the version I prefer.

'Homburg' (1967)

Personnel:
Gary Brooker: piano, vocals
Matthew Fisher: organ
David Knights: bass
B.J. Wilson: drums
Written by: Brooker, Reid
Recorded: March-June 1967, Olympic Studios, London, UK
Producer: Denny Cordell
Label: Regal Zonophone
Release date: September 1967 (UK)
Charts: UK: 6, US: 34
Length: 3:54

Tainted by scandal, they might be, but the band dutifully threw themselves onto the pop merry-go-round. While waiting for their debut album to hit the stores, they gave themselves the onerous task of following 'A Whiter Shade Of Pale', and since this was effectively their *first* release as the stable Trower/ Wilson band, they made sure the whole world noticed. The latter was hard with their static stage presence, all members sitting down to play. It led to the ridiculous vision of the band trying hard to look like serious musicians while dolled up in bright costumes.

But what to release? Reid nailed the dilemma succinctly in an interview with *Street Life* in 1976: 'At the time, we were oblivious, completely unaware. We never thought about the possible consequences of what we were doing. After 'Pale', our only thought was to come up with a single that would have been bigger. Somebody around us with more perspective could have seen that and suggested we follow up with something in a completely different direction, but still acceptable'.

Instead, and with hindsight disastrously, they opted for a song that seemed to have been forged from exactly the same crucible as 'Pale'. It had the same mesmerising tempo, grandiose keyboards, swirling imagery, and resolute lack of a contrasting middle eight, hence labelling themselves as their own copyists. Artistically, 'Homburg' is as strong and compelling a piece. But if you wanted to prove yourself to be a dynamic band in those volatile months of 1967, this was not the way.

Reid shrugged it all off in *Goldmine* in 2009: 'We were trying to outdo 'A Whiter Shade Of Pale', which in retrospect wasn't probably a great idea. We had it in our mind that we would do another slow tune, which was 'Homburg', which, you know, was somewhat reminiscent of 'A Whiter Shade Of Pale'. But we didn't really have a plan. We just were doing what we felt was natural and what we thought was right'.

Certainly, they moved fast, in the manner of the times. The Royer/Harrison lineup recorded 'Homburg' during the scrapped first album sessions, and it's this recording that was released. All the band did was turn down Royer's guitar so that it's inaudible (Trower didn't add new guitar; hence, again, he's not on a Procol Harum hit single) and obscure Harrison's drum track with an overdub by Wilson. You can still hear Harrison's fills in the background: a clattery undertow.

'Pale' was still in the UK top ten when, on 29 July, the *New Musical Express* reported that the next single would be 'Homburg Hat'. Fourteen days later, Penny Valentine in *Disc and Music Echo* had a copy to review. She enthused:

> Now, the main instrument is a cool piano, with that famous organ tucked firmly in the background and out of the way. The piano opens with gentle spring sounds and widens as Gary's voice comes cracking in with words that are even more evocative than 'Pale' – words that will remind you of wet leafy roads and tramps, strongly reminiscent of Samuel Beckett's *Waiting for Godot*, in fact.

Purchasers then had to wait another month while the band inked a deal with Regal Zonophone to get the thing out. This was bizarre or fortuitous, depending on how you interpret the events. EMI was a couple of years shy of launching its own progressive imprint Harvest, and in the meantime, the company thought it could remodel a label that had become all but synonymous with the Salvation Army as a vehicle for Denny Cordell's groups – meaning The Move and Procol Harum to begin with. The latter seem to have reacted to the shift by recording 'Magdalene': a parody of a Salvation Army anthem, as we'll see in the next chapter.

'Homburg' is certainly beguiling, and in a different way to the swooning lovesick party of 'Pale'. This is a long, dark night later, and the affair has ended for good, even if the protagonist still clings to it. Now everything's messed up to the point that his own body seems ill-fitted to his clothes, and everyday life offers not direction but obliteration. There are still the sneaky innuendos of 'Pale' – the many possible meanings of the word 'multilingual', all kinds of inferences in 'The lipsticked unmade bed' – but there's also an entire second verse occupied by the image of a stopped clock in the square outside. Should it shift, should the world presume to move forward again, then all will be lost. Against this bleakest of lyric, Brooker places a piano lament where every note drips heartache, while Fisher's primary contribution is a requiem effect in the choruses: the sound of the shutting of time.

The single was another UK success. Not *as* big, but respectable, and – we must assume – at least partly on its own merits. Let's not forget just how precipitously British music had expanded that year. When 'Pale' was released in May, it shouldered aside an acreage of mum-pop by the likes of The Tremeloes, Tom Jones, and Engelbert Humperdinck. When 'Homburg' first eased its way onto the *Melody Maker* chart at a lowly 30 on 7 October, it was up against the full flowering of psychedelic pop from

The Move, Traffic, Small Faces, and The Hollies ('King Midas In Reverse' was also a new entrant that week). Those hip young things in the mesmeric discotheques who didn't want *two* versions of 'Pale' in their collection had plenty of other choices. And yet the press bashed away. In November – long after 'Homburg' had risen into the top ten – *Beat Instrumental* scoffed about 'a constant cry that the Procol Harum was clearly a one-hit group'. The narrative was written full stop.

What was needed now was to crack the US as a touring band, which would guarantee them a future. To break in Trower and Wilson as a live act, Procol Harum followed the standard playbook of British bands in that period – they snuck off to Scandinavia, where they could iron out the kinks away from the scornful pens of the British weeklies. They finally made their way to the US in October, finding themselves in much the same post-hippie wilderness as Pink Floyd at the same time. (They even played on the same bill in San Francisco, alongside the similarly studious local band H. P. Lovecraft, whose 'The White Ship' most definitely had an effect on Reid.) Like the Floyd's, Procol Harum's trip was a disaster, but the US taught them the hard way how to extend their act to the required hour and a half or so: cycle everything around and around like 'Repent Walpurgis' to make the songs last as long as they could, and let Trower loose on extended blues solos whenever possible. Having ditched the costumes, minus Floyd's light-show gimmicks, and with no leaping about on stage or audience dancing in the aisles, Procol had to focus on the sound and the sound alone to carry the performance.

Given the apathy at home, it was a strategy that *had* to work, and it did. *Disc and Music Echo* seemed amazed by the success, reporting in November: 'There's nothing new or exciting about the stage presentation of Procol Harum. But the group is certainly producing sounds which have a positively spellbinding effect on audiences!'.

Even *Melody Maker* – quick to shove in the knife the moment a band was down – admitted there was something different about the group compared to 1967's increasingly elaborate pop vaudeville. In December, Chris Welch noted: 'Musically, they are not a particularly way-out group, and their cool, relaxed, trouble-free approach is almost like sanity in a sea of neurosis. No light shows, not particularly deafening, and practically static as regards stage presentation; somehow, they bring a magical touch to their live performances and records. It is believed this is achieved by singing and playing alone: a novel technique, not in common use'.

America continued to hold the band to its breast throughout their early years, even if Britain didn't care, and Procol Harum soon found themselves a huge audience in the US. By the end of 1968, they were high on the bill at the American festivals, including a turn at the massive Miami Pop Festival in December. It was only when the band signed to Chrysalis in 1970 and began to use British management that their home country belatedly began to realize the band did actually still exist.

'Good Captain Clack' (Brooker, Reid)

The first of Reid's nautical jaunts is a brief music-hall comedy number (running all of 1:29) that appeared on the 'Homburg' B-side and the UK edition of the first album, in near-identical form. (The discernible difference is the change from hi-hat to gong stroke after the line 'I'm content sipping lemon tea'.) The band barely keeps the rhythm together, while Fisher so enjoys his role as seafront fairground organist that uncomfortable intimations of Monty Python's Terry Jones come to mind.

Shine On Brightly (1968)

Personnel:
Gary Brooker: piano, koto, vocals
Matthew Fisher: organ, piano, vocals
David Knights: bass
Robin Trower: guitar, vocals
B.J. Wilson: drums
Recorded: 1967-1968, Advision, De Lane Lea and Olympic, London, UK
Producers: Denny Cordell, Tony Visconti
Label: A&M (US), Regal Zonophone (UK)
Release date: September 1968 (US), December 1968 (UK)
Charts: US: 24
Running time: 39:12 (A: 18:50, B: 20:22)

By the end of 1967, Keith Reid knew his share of grief. He'd already written two woozy, pain-laced hit singles on the subject of broken love affairs. Now, in the wake of the US tour (for which he acted as road manager), he found himself with another failed romance, and this, too, was destined to be a single.

While in New York, the band played the Greenwich Village nightclub Cafe Au Go Go. Wilson told *Melody Maker* that December: 'At the Cafe Au Go Go, you often get people coming out of the audience to play some jazz or sing. There was a fantastic girl called Sandy who just played piano and sang'.

Sandy Hurvitz, in fact, opened for the band. She'd been one of Frank Zappa's many girlfriends, had sung with The Mothers during their residency at The Garrick Theatre (in the same building as the Cafe Au Go Go), and had recorded an album for Zappa, belatedly released as *Sandy's Album Is Here At Last!* in 1968, with an oddly Procol-esque cat on the front. She later achieved success as the singer Essra Mohawk. Her affair with Reid was short but seems to have resonated painfully through a great deal of his work. The problem was that it's impossible to sustain a relationship with an ocean between you.

Reid first tried to distil his feelings in the song 'Quite Rightly So', the band's third single – at least he sent Hurvitz a copy of the lyric in March 1968 as if it was a personal message to her. It's likely its many opaque lines are private references we aren't expected to unravel. More importantly, you can imagine Reid, the romantic poet gazing out across the sea that separated him from his lover, casting his thoughts on perilous voyages and wretched Coleridge-style odysseys. Here was – perhaps – the genesis not just of the more obvious 'Too Much Between Us', but the undercurrent of songs like 'A Salty Dog' and 'Whaling Stories'.

From the very start of Reid's association with Procol Harum, we'd already seen how the sea tugged at his imagination, providing imagery that repeatedly cast him as a doomed sailor ('seasick' in 'Pale'). There's little poetic distance between the seabound virgins of 'Pale' and the pull of oblivion in 'Your Own Choice'. Perhaps it's hard to summon up romance for the Southend-on-Sea of the former or the dirty old river in the latter, on whose London bridges such thoughts are far from poetic. Better to think of the conquistador lying dead on the beach, the *Under Milk Wood*-evoking Captain Clack yearning for one more embarkation, the weeping figure on the dark shore of 'Magdalene', or the 'Amazon six-triggered bride' of 'A Christmas Camel'. Indeed, water itself is female in Reid's iconography, filled with mermaids and sirens, offering both escape and entrapment.

But what had been frivolous before – youthful wordplay or pastiche – now became deadly serious. Reid entered the deeps of his maturity on the cusp of the band's second album *Shine On Brightly*, and those deeps stretched down many fathoms. There were to be precious few frivolous songs like 'Mabel', at least not for several years.

But to begin with, the band were still in the whirl of their establishment. They continued to record doggedly. Much of *Shine On Brightly* was already coalescing before the US trip: a version of 'Magdalene' had been recorded, and sessions for the title track began in October. There were reports at the end of September that the band were to star in a movie to be called *Seventeen Plus*, as 'a pop group that becomes so powerful, it takes over the running of the country' according to *Disc and Music Echo*. It was also reported that Matthew Fisher would write his own album, and the band would create its *own* movie – which, to be fair, was exactly the same kind of bluster that Pink Floyd's press office had been issuing that same year.

Album sessions continued intermittently from December to April 1968, at which point it ought to have been possible to rush the album out to maintain momentum. The problem was that the first album had been so delayed that it was only now in British stores, and so this one was delayed too, and just as interminably. The only immediate evidence of the band's labour was the March release of the single 'Quite Rightly So', which hit a lowly 50 in the British charts and did nothing in America.

There were also problems in the studio, this time with the mono-obsessed Denny Cordell, who soon absconded to work on Joe Cocker's *With A Little Help From My Friends,* leaving assistant producer Tony Visconti and engineer Glyn Johns in charge. We're lucky Cordell left since his absence bequeathed us a stereo disc at last.

The most important decision made once Cordell was out of the room was to ditch several tracks and fill most of side two with an extended conceptual work – one of only two such works the band ever released. Parts of what was to become 'In Held 'Twas In I' were recorded as fragments in March and spliced together into a final suite by Visconti and Johns in April. Far more than the first album, the resulting disc was a sound world entirely the band's own – dark, haunted and despairing for sure, but also poised and majestic, a world unlike almost all the other progressive albums of 1968. The exceptions are Pink Floyd's *A Saucerful Of Secrets*, which was quite different but shared a similar glowering ambience, and Second Hand's *Reality,* which plumbed as deep a psychic trench.

However, with *Shine On Brightly* being a year or two ahead of the market that was to open for prog rock under its influence, the album wasn't an obvious commercial proposition. Brooker admitted to *Circus* in 1971: 'We recorded *Shine On Brightly* just for ourselves. We never thought anyone would want to hear it except maybe a few friends and others'.

'Pale' hadn't sold its millions to the gothic loners in ratty bedsits who gravitated around *A Saucerful Of Secrets* and *Reality*. Those buyers who still knew Procol Harum's name in 1968 had little interest in picking up *Shine On Brightly*, and if they did, the cover image soon had them slapping it back in the rack.

There were, in fact, two covers. One was a George Underwood painting, used for the UK and some other European countries, and a photograph that was used in the US and elsewhere. Underwood is better known as the painter of the extraordinary cover of the first Tyrannosaurus Rex album (released in July 1968 and also on Regal Zonophone). His cover to *Shine On Brightly* has little of that verve but merely illustrates the title track as clumps of hallucination around an oozing grand piano. The US version is far more evocative and is the definitive image of early Procol Harum. An armless, bald-headed, undressed shop mannequin, looking like it was rescued from a garbage heap, stands in front of a similarly battered upright piano in a desert, the whole thing heavily solarised to resemble a cross between the sea depths and the ugliest thrill of a nightmare. It's arresting, repugnant, and is a singular vision for a period in which Underwood-style paintings were commonplace (for example, see the ones Phil Travers created for The Moody Blues).

The liner notes were as striking as the US cover. They were written by Paul Williams of *Crawdaddy* and continued his campaign to shoehorn Procol Harum into the Dylan-to-Band narrative. 'Have you noticed how much the first Procol album (which was so influenced by *Blonde On Blonde*) influenced *Music From Big Pink*?', he wrote – a suggestion The Band categorically denied.

Reid told *Street Life* in 1976: 'I think we were probably one of the first groups to hear The Band because at one stage there was a possibility of Albert Grossman managing us when we started touring in America. We went up to his office and he told us about this new group called The Crackers, which is what The Band called themselves at the time. He played us a tape of their album, and that was after *Shine On Brightly*'. Most certainly, the last comment is wrong since *Music From Big Pink* was released first. If anything, there was a continuing influence the other way, which certainly makes sense given the Band-style pieces on *A Salty Dog* and *Home*. Reid opined to UCLA Radio in 1969 (reprinted – ironically – in *Crawdaddy* the same year) that it was Williams's inference that had offended the *Rolling Stone* reviewer who gave *Shine On Brightly* a poor review and that the band had nothing at all to do with the liner notes: 'We didn't even see them before the album came out'.

As a pointed postscript, an equally dismal 1971 review of *Broken Barricades* in the same paper quoted as hearsay Robbie Robertson's dismissal of the group: 'I've heard vaguely a few records by them, and they're still singing that same song'.

'Quite Rightly So' (Brooker, Fisher, Reid)

The cultural significance of 'Pale' notwithstanding, Procol Harum had nothing in common with the flower-power or hippie movements of 1967 and were almost unique in not having to adapt their music to the post-psychedelic landscape of 1968. The colour had gone out of London nightlife at the end of the summer. The situation with the US counterculture darkened daily. Procol Harum could never react to a style they were never truly a part of, but it's notable just how contrary *Shine On Brightly* is. When others were finding solace in returning to nature, frolicking in meadows, dancing with the gods of the woods, or digging into their folk traditions, *Shine On Brightly* was a resolutely urban album steeped in technological angst. Like its predecessor, there were no folk instruments or circle jams. At a time when The Beatles were getting mellow in Rishikesh, and The Incredible String Band and The Moody Blues were offering homespun Eastern philosophy, the album's use of sitar was intended as a sarcastic commentary on the very idea of a search for enlightenment, presenting it as silly and self-indulgent. There *are* answers, the album posited, but they're not easy, and you're not going to like them.

All the album's preoccupations are distilled into this opener, which purposefully fades in on Fisher's organ as if the band had never finished playing 'Repent Walpurgis', merely it cycled around and around in the background for all those months while you were elsewhere. Stereo enabled the band to open cinematically and to immerse you in what is actually Procol Harum's most drug-steeped album. It's mixed for the hallucinations, to borrow a Grateful Dead phrase, and like their contemporaneous *Anthem Of The Sun,* those hallucinations are predominantly dark, with seams of momentary joy flashing by like traffic streaks. The Dead, too, remained urban at this time, writing their album in praise of San Francisco. 'Quite Rightly So' is not so much a song of sorrow for a failed affair as a love song to New York and is the beginning of Reid's eventual decision to move permanently to the city.

The song climbs to the same brutal crescendos we'd witnessed on the first album, driven as much by Trower's fuzz blasts as Fisher's queasy Lowrey organ. But Fisher dominates the solo, playing the haunted version of a carnival barker's come-on that is Fisher's predominant style on the disc, while Trower manages no more than a few emphatic bleats in response. The fade eventually hauls the track back into the gloom from which it had arisen.

The lyric is Reid's usual catalogue of sickness and uncertainty (the only recurring trait it lacks is shame), with the repeated image of a wheat field that's alternatively so profuse that Reid is lost among its stalks and barren from lack of sunshine. (In context, it's clear that the field is a city, and the wheat its people.) The song declares that contradiction and confusion are all you can expect here. The only sure thing is the title: the answer to a question you're not privileged to hear.

'Shine On Brightly' (Brooker, Reid)
The title track erupts into life as if beginning in mid-performance. In the chorus, Trower and Fisher play a vicious vamp and Morse code staccato notes over Brooker's plunging piano chords and the band's rasping accompaniment. In the verses, Brooker beats time incongruously on his keys while trying to navigate Reid's awkward syntax, and Fisher plays spooky ascending counterpoint lines that disorientate the listener, building an intense psychosis that the chorus both resolves and heightens, offering the fixed grin of a hollow respite before the whole thing churns over again. Fisher's solo is an even more macabre version of his fairground organ sound, panned from speaker to speaker like a passing parade of grimacing goblins.

Reid's words are a barrage of unpleasant images and paranoid self-examination that take us through the disassociated fatalism of 'Homburg' (a ringing clock that won't stop, a missing signpost) and the nauseous swaying of 'Pale' to hideous intimations of grandeur cut violently short by the intrusion of a 'eunuch friend' and a spin around a circus of the damned. Reid admitted that he'd tried LSD by this time, and there is surely some of that crowded torrent of thought here: a funless trip in a darkened room.

The Italian single 'Il Tuo Diamante' grafts a different vocal performance onto a slightly different mix of the track. It's not a translation but a far inferior lyric by Italian poet Giulio Rapetti, who wrote under the name Ivan Mogul. 'Your diamond will shine', goes the chorus, 'but your heart will remain cold'. The credit reads 'Mogul/Brooker/Reid', though both Mogul's prominence and Reid's participation are debatable.

'Skip Softly (My Moonbeams)' (Brooker, Reid)
Having been ushered twice into the fairground of the soul, we now find ourselves on the sawdust of a circus tent: another place the album will revisit later. Though it's true that Fisher's coda steals from Aram Khachaturian's 'Sabre Dance', that's not actually relevant to what's happening here. Actually, we're witness to clowns tumbling out of the wings as our performance ends, and the music is just an aural cliché.

The song is jaunty but dislocated – the acrobatics of paraplegics – but it's of note for one likely influence and one probable coincidence. The influence was on Cockney Rebel's 'Mr. Soft', which borrowed the humorous trampoline rhythm, the baritone vocal and a word from the title, and was included on an album (*The Psychomodo*) which also used the circus as a metaphor for madness. The coincidence is the phrase 'stairs up to heaven'. It's certain that Jimmy Page had been listening to the band. He'd wanted to poach B. J. Wilson for his New Yardbirds, though what became Led Zeppelin was already finalised and touring by the time *Shine On Brightly* was released in September. It also seems possible that Page heard *Shine On Brightly* later since *Led Zeppelin II* uses the same title as 'Rambling On' and repeats that track's trick of fading out and in.

Apart from its circus ambience, 'Skip Softly' isn't much more than filler. Reid's lyric is perfunctory – a neutered speck of Dylan derision; its only memorable line is the last: 'I'd as soon talk to you as make love to a wall'. The song's dispatched in little more than a minute, after which everything else is an invocation of a kind we'll hear better on 'In Held 'Twas In I'. Still, the song is entertaining, and its title does signal a precipitous downward shift in the album's already bleak sound.

'Wish Me Well' (Brooker, Reid)
Trower was always a blues purist, to the point that it's usually hard to ascertain his involvement in any song that isn't a blues. As a consequence, the band indulged him in a straight blues every once in a while simply to give him a feature on stage. Later, he'd write those songs himself. For now, 'Wish Me Well' is the album's least affecting track: a maudlin gospel sing-along in which Reid affects his typical blues trick of moaning about his troubles. Our narrator is at rock bottom and declares that the only way out of his mental turmoil is suicide. Though it's not clearly stated, it infers he's going to throw *himself* down a wishing well. Whether true or not, 'I'm going down' is a clear forerunner of the hells of 'Juicy John Pink' and 'The Dead Man's Dream'.

There may not be much to this song, but a clotted, weighty production maintains interest in the performance. Brooker, Trower, and possibly others shout the words in unison, an uncredited Steve Winwood plays Hammond organ, and it's likely that other members of Traffic keep time on handclaps and tambourine since Wilson was apparently too sick to play. (Traffic were also at Olympic at the time, recording their eponymous second album.) Trower dutifully solos, though not with the same fire he'd demonstrated on the first album, and Brooker's cry 'Sock it to me/Sock it to me Robin!' seems like it's trying too hard in the quest for excitement that the song doesn't deliver.

'Rambling On' (Brooker, Reid)
The last track on side one is only 4:28 in length, but it's the album's longest individual song and is something of an epic. From its blustery stop-start opening to the 'Strawberry Fields Forever' fade out and in again, it seems windblown, airy, insubstantial. And yet the band's sound is massive and unwieldy, far too fat to fly. This is all surely purposeful.

The piece began with Reid's most hefty lyric since 'Pale' – four dense verses without a chorus – which describe his character's inspiration (from watching 'a *Batman* movie', which presumably means the 1966 Adam West comedy rather than the 1940s serials) to get a pair of wings and take to the skies. A crowd gathers to watch him jump off a tall building, one of them admonishing him that he's not an angel and, therefore, would be doomed to fail. Our protagonist winks that off, the ludicrous notion that he has 'barbells on my eyelids' implying that this isn't so much a chance to fly as an attempt to test the beneficence of God. He raises his voice in hymn and the crowd dutifully sings along. Finally, a gust of wind sends him soaring. He heads off toward 'the golden gates' (which could mean the pearly gates rather than the Golden Gate bridge or the Golden Gate in Jerusalem) and plummets Icarus-like to Earth. The collision should have killed him instantly, but he emerges unscathed, hence succeeding in his test.

Brooker savoured putting this sly and witty tale to music. He told *Goldmine* in 2021: 'With the words I got from Reid, I was able to throw myself into them. I'd get pictures. With 'Rambling On', I actually do see somebody standing on the edge of a 20-storey building, with this terrible kite on, expecting to jump off and fly'.

The result is wonderful – a heartful silliness set to Brooker's best classical chords and a jabbing, beautifully poised accompaniment from Trower and Wilson in particular.

'Magdalene (My Regal Zonophone)' (Brooker, Reid)
We might have considered this a reaction to Reid's breakup with Sandy Hurvitz, particularly given that it indulges in exactly the same kind of wordplay as 'Quite Rightly So', except it was already written, and a take was recorded before Reid went to America. In fact, the original 1967 version of 'Magdalene' (abandoned when the master tape was wiped, but of which an acetate survives and has been released) is identical to this one in sound, lyric, and structure, right down to the cries of the title in the coda.

In retrospect, the very idea that a song this dirge-like could have been a hit seems absurd. It's a prospective B-side for sure, and perhaps could have even been on the back of 'Homburg'. It would have appealed to Brooker and Reid's sense of humour to instigate their career on Regal Zonophone with a parody of a Salvation Army song, and 'Magdalene' was carefully written to sound that way. Nor did side two of *Shine On Brightly* need the song. The album would have worked just as well (and been even more iconic) had 'In Held 'Twas In I' filled the entire side. But there's something so comfortably dispiriting about 'Magdalene' that it's impossible to think of the disc without it sitting there, glacial, inert and hag-haunted, thanklessly plunging the listener into the side's cold, lifeless water.

Unlike the band's other comedy numbers and pastiches (including 'Skip Softly' and 'Wish Me Well'), the song is played with genuine respect, and no studio chatter has emerged to even hint that there's off-screen laughter once its parping pretend trumpets have finally ceased, or that Reid's stumbling lyric – all love-song stereotype and self-correction – is meant as satire. Quite the opposite. We hear Reid in the wake of a relationship, fighting to make sense of his feelings in exactly the same way John Lennon does in 'Strawberry Fields Forever' – so much so that Reid can't even decide on his trademark shame. 'Unashamed' tears have turned, just two lines later, into a 'shame I found too painful'. It all makes sullen sense. Who hasn't been there, in the chill of that beach? The tune is so beguiling, and the band's rendition so beautiful that what could have been another throwaway is actually one of the album highlights.

'In Held 'Twas In I' (Brooker, Fisher, Reid)
The band didn't intend to create an epic. Such things didn't exist in rock at the time. When they began to piece together what became this suite, they didn't even know what their goal was. They simply wanted to pull together some fragments they'd already written (the same reason The Beatles created the medley on *Abbey Road* a year later) and see where their imagination could take them. Reid told UCLA Radio in 2002: 'We wanted to do an extended piece, and we also wanted to involve Matthew Fisher in writing some music. It was actually the wanting to include Matthew in writing that was one of the reasons we did that piece'.

There was never a map, like how Pink Floyd pinned up graph paper in the studio to determine the structure and dynamics of 'A Saucerful Of Secrets' at the same time Procol Harum were recording this. 'In Held 'Twas In I' had more in common with Frank Zappa's side-length suites on *Absolutely Free* – simply an organic accumulation of songs segued with clever links, one piece leading to the next, and (another trick The Beatles were to repeat) an ending reprise of something you'd heard earlier to make it all seem intentional. Reid told *Goldmine* in 2009: 'We didn't actually envisage that it would be 18 minutes. It took on a life of its own, and one piece led to another, and we composed it in the way it appears. So just one piece grew out of the other, both musically and lyrically, and eventually, 18 minutes later, we got to the end'.

Despite this, it's likely the band knew how much space they had to fill and that the finished piece is 17:29 because that's what they needed. It certainly couldn't have been much longer.

This process of linking fragments together was dangerous, to say the least. Recording each part separately and then leaving Tony Visconti to assemble the tapes into a master could have easily resulted in something malformed and chaotic. It seems to be mere serendipity that it actually worked and that it worked so well that many later progressive rock acts (starting with Van der Graaf Generator and Genesis) were to use it as the template for their own big statements. Brooker explained to *Creem* in 1972: 'All the ideas were there, but it wasn't completely written before we started to record it. I think we'd written about half of it before we started to record it, and the other bits came as we went along. It's so long that we never knew what was going to happen until we finally finished it. It was put together, and we played it one night through the big studio speakers. We were lying around on our backs'.

Van der Graaf Generator told exactly the same tale of the composition of 'A Plague Of Lighthouse Keepers'.

Like the Beatles' medley, 'In Held 'Twas In I' never really had a name. The final title is simply the first word of each of its five vocal sections (which do not correspond to its divisions), a meaningless concatenation of fragments that awkwardly reveals the track's piecemeal nature. There was an antecedent for this. Donovan had created the title of his 1966 hit 'Sunshine Superman' from the first word of its first two verses, accidentally creating an iconic phrase. You surely can't say the same of the gloopy title 'In Held 'Twas In I', which is neither evocative nor surprising, and any story you impose on those random words (for example, I tend to see it as a trip through hell) is in your own mind. Just like 'Pale', 'In Held 'Twas In I' is open to endless interpretations, all or none of which might be true. The likelihood is none, given that there wasn't a plan, but Brooker had his own explanation that he related to *Prog* magazine in 2018: 'It's got a lot of strange pieces that we knitted together, but you can get some kind of story out of it. It starts off with the beginning of the universe, really, if that's possible. There's some Buddhist chant, and it ends up going to Heaven. It's even got drug addiction in the middle'.

The divisions – dutifully transcribed on every release of the track – are handy signposts through the maze of the piece but have survived mostly for publishing purposes. Despite this, there are no individual writing credits for these divisions, even though we can pin different sections to different writers. For example, Fisher was largely responsible for the final section 'Grand Finale'. It also seems that Trower contributed the alarming guitar riff slotted into that long undocumented stretch between 'In The Autumn Of My Madness' and 'Look To Your Soul', and he doesn't get a credit at all.

Brooker's recitation in the opening section 'Glimpses Of Nirvana' suggests we're about to be taken on a journey toward enlightenment – a notion many Procol Harum fans would surely reject since it places the band much too close to The Moody Blues, who were also stringing tracks into long suites that needed to be listened to in order, and whose album *In Search Of The Lost Chord* (released two months before *Shine On Brightly*) was on the exact same theme. It had a similar cover to the British version of *Shine On Brightly*, mixed singing and spoken sections, and the opening drone that Brooker called 'the beginning of the universe' is just like the effects the Moodies used to introduce their albums. It's better to think of 'In Held 'Twas In I' as the struggle to survive a long dark night of the soul. Indeed, this recitation has all Reid's trademark beats: it's cruelly introspective, accusing its narrator of 'wallowing in a morass of self-despair'. Reid's persona states that the only way to survive the crumbling away of reality is to try to talk about it.

Brooker then relates the bitterly humorous tale of a spiritual pilgrim who spends five years meditating on the meaning of life before being granted an audience with the Dalai Lama – the fount of all wisdom – who fobs him off with a homily. Reid admitted he simply repeated a joke he'd been told by a friend in a London cafe. The point seems to be that you won't find answers from religious figures since they know as little as you do. So much for Rishikesh. And so much for *In Search Of The Lost Chord*, which reaches a conclusion that 'In Held 'Twas In I' ridicules here in its opening minutes. By the way, the twangy accompaniment to the Dalai Lama tale is not a Tibetan instrument but a Japanese koto played by Brooker.

A thunderous rock interval (apparently written by Fisher) evokes being slapped across the head repeatedly with a monk's wooden paddle. At 2:04, there's a surprising mournful sequence in which an uncredited sitar player stabs what's left of these pretensions, a mock Gregorian choir pokes the corpse a few times, and Brooker plays a beautiful requiem on piano. It's hard to believe, given all this, that things are going to get a lot darker before the mood lightens again: we're a long way from midnight yet. The second recitation – also part of 'Glimpses Of Nirvana' – is spoken by Reid himself and admits to doubts about the whole God thing and how it's even worse for him *not* to believe than to fall back on the easy comfort of faith. What *is* there left to guide you in a mechanical universe?

We'll find out later, but first, we must explore this mechanical universe to the very cogs of its clockwork. At 4:29, a tubular bell strikes the hour – 13 – and shoves us like an acid-dazed defendant into the cosmic trial of ''Twas Teatime At The Circus' – a piece that ought to be a comic interlude like Genesis's 'Willow Farm' in 'Supper's Ready' but is actually even more grim than the start. Our star act is 'King Jimi', a reference to the fact that even in 1968, it was obvious that Hendrix was a freak show: a clown lashed by his management into performing empty tricks for his audience. There's more of the organ evocation of 'Skip Softly', this time with the expected screamer march 'Entrance Of The Gladiators' by Julius Fučík.

A rather unconvincing crowd roars approval at 5:42, but this is immediately swallowed up in the earth-shattering explosion that starts 'In The Autumn Of My Madness', a plunge into true horror. A double-tracked Fisher sings yet more of Reid's scarified self-doubt, this time with the intimation (true, as it turned out) that he would eventually have nothing more to say and would likely end his days old and bitter and no closer to answers than now. The band's brutal rock accompanies Fisher, peppered with fearsome noises and lost-soul screams. It's like 'Pale' after the party gets *really* macabre. Brooker's voice in this maelstrom is actually him singing the 'Homburg' chorus with the tape reversed.

An alarming splice at 8:56 boots us deeper still into Trower's infernal riff, the plodding approach of something monstrous, and a reprise of the sitar melody from 'Glimpses Of Nirvana' refracted into punishing proto-heavy metal. It's only the introduction of a harpsichord to open 'Look To Your Soul' at 10:56 that offers any kind of handle on all this abuse, and by now, the listener is fully traumatised and huddled in a psychic corner, hoping for any form of solace. Even a speck of it would do, and a speck is all Reid's lyric offers. There are no answers, he says. You'll simply have to trust in your soul and carry on. Whether this assuages the spiritual doubt that was the whole point of the journey is debatable. There's no proof of God here, no suggestion that religion is any better than physics, except that it prevents you from feeling quite so bad about death. But still, Reid concludes that it's a 'crime' to disbelieve. Ultimately, he tells us, 'the lesson lies in learning', which seems to suggest that it's the five years of contemplation that matters, not whatever it was the Dalai Lama said. *Faith* is the point, not the truth of that belief.

'Look To Your Soul' culminates at 13:14 in a triumphal Trower guitar solo and fades to silence at 13:55, the point where you might assume the suite should end. Instead, there are another three and a half minutes of Fisher's 'Grand Finale' – a virtual rewrite of 'Repent Walpurgis' that hits all the same pomp beats and electric fanfares, accompanied by a wordless choir of whatever friends and wives could be corralled into the studio that day. Trower solos again (though not as well as on 'Walpurgis'), and the choir once more lifts the roof to celestial heights.

'In The Wee Small Hours Of Sixpence' (Brooker, Reid)
The B-side to 'Quite Rightly So' is certainly not something you'd want infringing on the album. It's not fast, but it has the same breezy feel as much of *A Whiter Shade Of Pale* and has a rambling, inconsequential lyric about 'a rusty old retainer' mourning his absent master (a knight away at war) with wordplay about a rusty sword that's nevertheless 'blunt as sharp enough'. Not even Fisher's nimble organ interjections can bring life to the piece. Trower sits it out, and nobody's thought of a worthwhile break. Brooker himself later rubbished the track, considering it a half-hearted attempt to put a tune to a bad set of words.

A Salty Dog (1969)

Personnel:
Gary Brooker: piano, celeste, guitar, tubular bells, harmonica, recorder, vocals
Matthew Fisher: organ, marimba, guitar, piano, recorder, vocals
David Knights: bass
Robin Trower: electric and acoustic guitars, tambourine, vocals
B.J. Wilson: drums, percussion
Recorded: January-March 1969, EMI Studios, London, UK
Producer: Matthew Fisher
Label: A&M (US), Regal Zonophone (UK)
Release date: April 1969 (US), July 1969 (UK)
Charts: US: 32, UK: 27
Running time: 40:34 (A: 21:17, B: 19:17)

In 1969, Procol Harum were finally in a good place commercially and artistically. Their lineup had bedded in, and they recognized their strengths, which were now considerable. *Shine On Brightly* had enabled them to create an image that moved away from 'Pale': a millstone still, but a less onerous burden to carry. The unique circumstances of their record deal meant they had control of their product. Among other benefits, if Reid's relationship with Dickinson had taken a knock in 1968, it was finally back on course and she was again the band's designer. Procol Harum were altogether more confident as performers and writers and willing to take risks. The shared duties on 'In Held 'Twas In I' meant the songwriting and singing were no longer restricted to Brooker, though Reid continued to write all the words. *A Salty Dog* was to be the first true test of what they could do, and many fans and commentators rate it as their finest work.

Single success was still seemingly a thing of the past. The title track ought to have been a massive hit, but it did next to nothing in either the UK or US. But the market that had opened for adult, progressive rock meant singles were now mostly promotional tools. The album was the statement, the album was the thing that students would buy, and albums like *A Salty Dog* were intended as definitive experiences to be listened to in one sitting, beginning to end. Albums lived or died not just on their highs but on the absence of filler and on having a unified sonic landscape into which listeners immersed themselves with full attention.

For this, you needed to sweat the small stuff. *A Salty Dog* was a leap forward for Procol Harum in that it was recorded on eight-track, allowing far more sophistication in its production and at a slightly less hurried and piecemeal rate than the previous two albums. Having been mostly written while touring the US in 1968, the band first attempted to record it at A&M Studios in Los Angeles but gave up with nothing but the B-side 'Long Gone Geek' in usable form. There was a much more amenable atmosphere at Abbey Road, where engineers were willing to let the band experiment and raid the

EMI sound effects library and instrument cupboard. And the album was self-produced, with Fisher's duties obviating the possibility of yet more outside meddling.

It also benefitted from the impression it gave of being a conceptual work, even if this was mostly due to Reid's constantly regurgitated syllabus of tropes and the striking front cover on which Dickinson presented Reid mocked-up as a grizzled sailor laughing mirthlessly in a parody of the Player's Navy Cut cigarette packet (a type of twisted tobacco first targeted at sailors). Nautical imagery was sprinkled throughout the disc. Three songs were about sea voyages. Others suggested 'In Held 'Twas In I' journeys of the mind: a churn of desperate introspection that seemed as claustrophobic as the inside of a ship's cabin. Coleridge, again, was the closest analogy, given how haunted the entire album sounds. There's no levity on *A Salty Dog*, and even its one flippant track, 'Boredom', curdles the mood from the title downward.

The sheer diversity of approaches ought to have made the album seem muddled. That it did the opposite is a testament to some indefinable Procol Harum spirit that infuses every piece regardless of its writers or style. As Gary Brooker succinctly told *Melody Maker* in June 1969: 'The music stays the same. It's just going out in branches'. Fisher had his own theory, as related to *Record Mirror* in August: 'The only thing that is constant so far is that we tend to do things that are rather slow. It wasn't intended that way. It's the result of the words. The way Keith writes doesn't lend itself to fast treatment'.

The use of strings also unified the disc. This wasn't the first time Procol Harum had recorded with orchestral instruments (Tony Visconti had added solemn, sometimes astringent strings and woodwinds to the first album outtake 'Understandably Blue' in 1967), and it seemed a natural progression from merely quoting classical-style works on piano and organ to actually incorporating establishment sounds. But *A Salty Dog* stood out in a year when a number of other progressive acts were trying to incorporate an orchestra live or on an album (including The Nice, Deep Purple, and Pink Floyd) by the simple fact that the album's string arrangements were actually very good. They sounded neither amateur nor pretentious, and their careful distribution on just three tracks ensured they didn't swamp the work. Moreover, they formed a balance and counterpoint to Trower's increasingly dominant guitar work, which was still restricted to the blues but seemed to get heavier with every album. The title track gains all the plaudits, but it's the sudden startling conceptual wrench from 'Juicy John Pink' to 'Wreck Of The Hesperus' that defines the album.

In the summer, the band bowed to the inevitable and took their highbrow/lowbrow convergence to the stage. On 6 July, they appeared with the Stratford Festival Orchestra at the Shakespeare Festival in Canada. Reid told *Zigzag* in 1973: 'The idea was that there would be an orchestra come on and play for whatever it was, 20 minutes or half an hour, and then we would play with the orchestra for half an hour, followed by another half hour on our own. We did that, playing songs from *A Salty Dog* and the whole of 'In Held 'Twas In I', and we wanted to record that, but due to – I think – union troubles, we were unable to do so'.

In 2020, Brooker recalled to *SongwriterUniverse* how he scrambled to find music that would fit:

Somebody there thought that Procol Harum should play with a big orchestra, so they took it upon themselves to book us there. So we were going to play with this orchestra, and all we've got is 'A Salty Dog'. So that was when I thought: 'What about 'In Held 'Twas In I'? It's got the length. You could really do something with an orchestra with that'. Anyway, it took me a few weeks and I worked on it quite hard. I was in San Francisco at the time, having a bit of a break, so I rented a nice grand piano. I wrote all the parts. There was also going to be a choir at Stratford, so I had to give them some bits, so I did that as well.

The band might have thought it an encouraging experiment, but the press excoriated them. Writing in *The Spectator*, Lorne Betts sneered: 'Unfortunately, the Procol Harum have no conception of rhythm and its immense possibilities. There was nothing but an incessant pounding of drums and cymbals in a vain effort to cover the inadequacy of rhythm, form and even material'.

In the Toronto *Telegram*, Kenneth Winters was even more willing to brutalise young people for having the nerve to try something new with the classical stage:

Yesterday's attempt – though it exhausted the box office and had its mammoth and stubbornly innocent audience howling like dogs – was about as tin-eared and hollow-headed a rumpus as I can ever remember having sat through to the pitiful end. In two gruesome mishmashes compounded of classical-melodic tag-ends, night club piano procedures, muddled verse, soap-operatic religiosity and funeral-parlour solemnity, the Procul Harum and the Festival Orchestra joined idioms for what may have been a half-hour but seemed an eternity.

Never has that wearying misspelling seemed so spiteful. But the greatest dissent was internal. Trower needed to turn down his amp so that he didn't drown out the acoustic players, and this rankled him so much that he refused to allow the band to do any more live work with an orchestra. But watch this space.

All must have seemed stable and well when *A Salty Dog* (again, a little belatedly) was readied for UK stores in July. But disaster continued to hamstring the band. Knight wanted out, and Fisher was sick of touring and yearned to concentrate on production. Both quit before the release. Other cracks were showing with Trower, whose devotion to straight blues was beginning to sit uneasily against all the new possibilities the album was opening up for the band.

'A Salty Dog' (Brooker, Reid)

Eerie, mysterious, as chilly as Coleridge's *The Rime Of The Ancient Mariner*, laced through with old whaling tales and the rum-soaked ravings of sailors teetering on rotting wharves, 'A Salty Dog' both distils many of Reid and Brooker's obsessions to that date and flings wide the band's sound world. Even with words this strong and an orchestral arrangement this adept, the piece would be nothing without the solid core of its melody, which is also a leap forward for its writer. Brooker explained to UCLA Radio in 2001 how he got the idea for the tune:

> It was one of those songs that just tumbled from the sky. I was sitting down at a piano somewhere – I think it was in Switzerland – and this train went past and made a noise as they do, and this happened to be three notes. I thought: 'What's that? That's a strange cluster of notes'. And I found it on the piano in the same key and everything, and I just stabbed away at it and then I made it sound slightly nicer. And that's the start of 'Salty Dog'. And then, within a few minutes, that song was written.

He told *Songfacts* in 2010 that this was one of the tracks where he already had the music when Reid sent lyrics to match: 'I think soon after I got that idea, Keith sent me the words, and they just seemed to fit with it very, very easily'.

From Reid's perspective, it was the other way around. He told UCLA Radio in 2002: 'I remember 'A Salty Dog' being one where I'd given him the lyric, and then sometime later he said, 'I've written something for this' and played it for me, and it was nothing like I had imagined it at all'. The germ of Reid's verses was a piece of graffiti he happened to see in a Boston bar: 'Great God skipper, we've run aground'. Like the phrase that prompted 'Pale', it took Reid into a reverie in which he concocted a scenario around it, though the phrase never appears in the song. Being the reminiscence of a survivor of a disastrous voyage (much like Herman Melville's Ishmael in *Moby-Dick*), the words chart the ship's straying off the psychic map into the hallucinated waters beyond, at the beck and call of a captain maddened with determination. They wash up on an alien shore, destroy the ship to prevent the temptation to ever try to leave, and settle there. Eventually, all the others die, leaving only the narrator to set down his verses for future eyes.

The total effect is like a found object: a message in a bottle. It needed a musical treatment as strange as its words. In 2020, Brooker told *SongwriterUniverse* about his thought processes in detail: 'I had the tune over the top, and I didn't really see what else could be in it. I couldn't see rock guitar in it at all, and at the time, I didn't hear organ in it. But I thought some strings would be good'. How, then, to score it? Brooker had no formal training as an orchestral arranger. But the previous March, Procol Harum had toured Germany in support of The Bee Gees, whose act integrated a pop group and a large string section, and Brooker had become friendly with one of the viola players. Brooker continued:

> I went around to see him and I asked him how I could do it. He told me that violas and violins have different ranges, of course, and you write within those ranges. And where the instruments sound like you want them to sound, that's where you put it, in notes. So I soon got the idea that you've got two violins – the first violin and the second violin – and the violas, cellos and basses. So I got out this book I had which gave the range of instruments. The violas were suddenly complicated, because it's written in the alto clef. It's not like looking at piano music.

Having written his arrangement, Brooker assembled a small group of orchestral players at Abbey Road and gave himself the reckless task of conducting them:

> I put my hand down to start counting the time, and they were all late. I said: 'Come on, come on, wake up, boys'. You know, conducting is a little bit different from rock. So anyway, the leader of the orchestra said: 'Don't worry about it, Gary. You just count. We've got the tempo. You count us in and we'll be all right'. So I just gave them the 1-2-3, and off they went. And they knew exactly what to do. They played it wonderfully.

The result remains perhaps the definitive Procol Harum statement – again, *that single* notwithstanding – and one of the band's most loved pieces. Brooker's taste and restraint, the extraordinary decision of the orchestral players to actually work with him rather than sleepwalk through the session, Wilson's majestic fills, careful touches such as seagull sound effects and having band roadie John 'Kellogs' Kalinowski blow a bosun's whistle at the appropriate moment, and of course Brooker singing one of Reid's most beguiling lyrics, make the track a standout achievement and a slam-dunk as a hit single. Needless to say, it climbed no higher than 44 in the UK and didn't even chart in the US.

'The Milk Of Human Kindness' (Brooker, Reid)
An underdeveloped blues, this track's only notable feature is Brooker's use of the studio's detuned upright piano, likely the same 'Mrs Mills piano' that the Beatles had used on 'Penny Lane' and other songs. The title's lift from Shakespeare may have been unconscious, given that the lyric is earthy and mundane. In a characteristic mix of spite and self-pity, Reid complains about

the actions of someone who took advantage of a mistake, stomping him further into the dirt. Trower squalls fuzz guitar all over the song, but the tune is not memorable and the track outstays its welcome.

'Too Much Between Us' (Brooker, Trower, Reid)

This lilting ballad is the most delicate thing Procol Harum ever recorded, and the music is a fitting complement to Reid's most fragile lyric. For once, all the guards are down, and his words are direct enough for us to unravel them. The singer is separated from the one he loves by an ocean and a sufficient time zone difference for her to be sleeping while he's up writing the message. The use of the word 'ratings' makes it seem like he's on a ship, though if this is truly a requiem for Sandy Hurvitz, it's just misdirection. The usual emotions are here: uncertainty, wordlessness, shame, regret, fatalism. The gulf of the sea is a metaphor for a gulf of silence, and there's no return to land.

The track barely rouses from its musical bed of softly picked acoustic guitar, pillowy tuned percussion, and Fisher's most spectral organ-playing. Reid's proxy in this – as in all his other emotions – is Brooker, who sings with genuine feeling. The crown of this most sorely overlooked treasure is Fisher's languid weaving solo in the fade, which channels similar work by Pink Floyd's Richard Wright.

'The Devil Came From Kansas' (Brooker, Reid)

The album's most muscular piece is a perplexing rage against something that has riled Reid and caused him to scatter vitriol like Catherine wheel sparks. Little is penetrable. I could perhaps make the case that 'There's a monkey riding on my back' is a reference to drugs, but what's all this business with the cheese and silver paper, and why is the singer again on his way to commit suicide? 'I am not a humble pilgrim', he remonstrates – a particularly fierce statement of self-denial given that there's a great deal of the 'In Held 'Twas In I' spiritual quest in *A Salty Dog,* which even ends with a song called 'Pilgrim's Progress'.

Our inability to make a coherent story from the lyric may simply be because there isn't one. Reid explained to *New Musical Express* in 1975: 'That came about simply because I've always liked Randy Newman. I bought his first album. There was a song on it called 'The Beehive State', a line about the senator from somewhere or other. That line inspired it'. But Reid misheard the line, turning 'the delegate from Kansas' into the title phrase.

Brooker enfolds the lyric in slamming piano chords and a furious stately chorus in which everyone in the room roars out the words. Trower slashes at his strings, and Wilson kicks all hell out of his drum kit. Wild stereo tricks – including a delay on Brooker's voice and wanton panning on Trower's solos – create a disorienting whirlwind, exacerbated by the song's jolting five-accent introduction and soggy mix. The result may sound like a drunk trying to knock down a courthouse by beating his head against it, but 'The Devil Came From Kansas' has a rousing squalor that sure does make you want to join in beside him.

'Boredom' (Fisher, Brooker, Reid)

With a tropical rhythm and the band all swapped around on whatever instruments they could drag out of the Abbey Road cupboard, 'Boredom' belies its title and Reid's despondent lyric (half John Lennon indecision, half heartless dismissal by a doctor who doesn't expect the patient to improve) by bringing something close to fun to the album. Brooker told *classicrockpage.com* in 2000: 'Matthew was the originator of the idea in the first place, and I think it's one of those great, well not particularly great, but one of those studio recordings where you take advantage of what's around, which in that case meant that we got our recorders out, we found a marimba or xylophone or something in the studio and just used some different instruments'.

It *is* great, at least from this listener's viewpoint, and so infectiously ramshackle that you can't help grinning along. I could imagine it as a real treat on a Faces or Humble Pie album. That it's *Procol Harum* makes it twice as delicious. Fisher gets to sing it while Brooker leans into the microphone for the chorus. The others all skip around Fisher's acoustic guitar in a self-consciously jolly campfire sing-along in a clearing in the ice-cold midnight woods.

'Juicy John Pink' (Trower, Reid)

Side two begins with a feature for Trower, consisting merely of his heavy blues guitar in straight emulation of his heroes, with Brower providing a rudimentary vocal and harmonica accents. The pair didn't even go to Abbey Road to perform it, recording the track raw in the Rolling Stones basement rehearsal room in Bermondsey Street in London's Docklands. *Crawdaddy* quoted Trower in 1969: 'It's us trying to get a really dirty Muddy Waters-type sound. It was recorded in a friend's basement with two old microphones and Gary standing about ten feet away. The name isn't any mysterious English pun. When Keith and I had written it, we thought it should be recorded on Blue Horizon and that we'd call the artist Juicy John Pink'.

Reid's lyric variation on the old 'Woke up this morning and found myself dead' line is surely parody, but Brooker sings it with verve, and there's punk power in Trower's tone. Still, 'Juicy John Pink' is another diversion, the musical antithesis of 'Boredom' but part of the same need to go 'out in branches'.

'Wreck Of The Hesperus' (Fisher, Reid)

The curious thing about this second orchestral piece is that it forms a counterpoint to 'A Salty Dog' but was born of a quite different mood on a quite different ocean. Whereas 'A Salty Dog' evokes the chilly Atlantic seas off the coast of Boston, 'Wreck Of The Hesperus' was inspired while Fisher and Reid were staying in San Francisco. It may nevertheless be a whaling tale if Reid has the *Essex* in mind, rammed and sunk by a sperm whale in the Pacific. There is, of course, also a link to Longfellow's poem 'The Wreck of the Hesperus' (about a ship lost in a storm off the coast of Massachusetts), but Reid's lyric is another Coleridge voyage, populated by the coffins, funerals, and cemeteries that were to become familiar on the *Home* album. It's an opaque calamity that befalls this vessel, not a physical storm but a psychic horror, and it has a great deal more power than Longfellow's rather mannered verse, even if it's a hopeless task to figure out the meaning of the refrain 'Burnt by fire, blind in sight, lost in ire'.

Fisher chose to accompany these words with tumbling piano arpeggios maintained for the entire three-minute running time, making the piece exhausting to hear and a chore to reproduce live. Consequently, it's not nearly as feted as 'A Salty Dog', and that's a shame, for Fisher indulges in an orchestral arrangement that's also the antithesis of Brooker's song – an apocalyptic whirl of psychotic brass and strings that swell constantly and eventually submerge the entire piece in such ludicrous pomp that you can imagine the players all tilting crazily on a creaking orchestra stage and jabbing each other with their bows. It sure does brighten up the otherwise rather flat side two. *Crawdaddy* quoted Fisher in 1969: 'When I wrote 'The Hesperus', I didn't have any orchestration in mind. When I arranged it for the orchestra, I included the Wagnerian bit simply because it happened to come into my mind at a time when I was looking for something that fit in that particular place. It just sounded appropriate, so in it went'.

To add to the piece's portrait of spume-flecked insanity, Brooker intimated that there might be some backwards piano in the piece, linking it to the similarly crazed sound world of 'In The Autumn Of My Madness'. He told *Contemporary Keyboard* in 1978: 'We used recordings of the piano played backwards on a lot of tracks so that a crescendo can be accented by the long, sustained chord played in reverse. We did that definitely on 'Wreck Of The Hesperus' and 'The Mark Of The Claw', and maybe on 'In Held 'Twas In I''.

As notable are Trower's keening guitar accents and a Wilson who seems determined to play as far behind the beat as he can, suggesting not so much drumming itself but the blowing echo of drums flung back by a wall of approaching water. Surprisingly, there's also a bedrock of acoustic guitar for the third time on the album from a band that had previously never bothered with the instrument, but you could hardly call the song folk.

'All This And More' (Brooker, Reid)
Madness also flavours this workmanlike track – a patent Procol Harum slow blues with that now-standard trick of alternating subdued verses with triumphal staircase-climbing choruses. There's even a brief pause for a classical piano motif. At the end, Brooker throws in a rudimentary brass arrangement over Trower's vicious one-note solo.

It may all seem perfunctory, but Reid claimed the lyric had personal significance, so there are evidently hidden depths in such superficial self-justification as 'If at times my nonsense rhymes/Then I'll stand trial' and the (again, now-characteristic) self-pity of 'I'm not so well these days'. It may merely mean that the 'you' of the chorus is the shelter of a lover, presumably Dickinson. Meanwhile, physical distance twins it to 'Too Much Between Us', while mention of 'whirlpools' and 'harbour lights' echo 'The Wreck Of The Hesperus' (forming a neat link in that Hesperus is the morning star: an image repeated here) and provide added ammunition for those who believe *A Salty Dog* is a thematic album. You get extra points if you mention that 'Maddox' is a reference to the legendary Welsh sailor who discovered America centuries before Columbus, but good luck working 'Lollard' into your theme.

'Crucifiction Lane' (Trower, Reid)
In common with his Jewish lyricist heroes – in particular Bob Dylan and Randy Newman, though the most obvious example is surely Paul Simon – Reid occasionally referenced the New Testament, and he had already questioned the veracity of Christ in the spoken section of 'Glimpses Of Nirvana'. 'Crucifiction Lane' seem to be an even more blatant attack, disagreeably punning 'fiction' into 'crucifixion' as if nobody had *actually* been executed in Jerusalem. One of the few things we can say for sure about the historical Jesus is that he *was*. It may simply be an ill-judged joke on Crucifix Lane in London, a road intersecting with Bermondsey Street. Not that any of this matters to the song, which is essentially a repeat of 'All This And More' only even more sour. Reid told *Melody Maker* in 1973: 'That was a picture of me and how I was feeling at that time. As it happened, the song went under the carpet and didn't work out well'.

The problem is mainly Reid's, given that he gave Trower little to work with. There's yet more self-pity and there's yet more of those nautical references: a whole couplet about ships and the sea. But the predominant mood is defensive. Just like The Moody Blues' 'Never Comes The Day' from *On The Threshold Of A Dream* (coincidentally, recorded and released at the same time as *A Salty Dog*), Reid warns that if only we knew what was inside him, we wouldn't want him around. If Trower can't pretty up these sentiments, he can make them starker still, which he does on these five long minutes of smouldering slow blues with a rasping vocal that seems out of place even among the album's multitude of voices and a long and not particularly memorable solo.

'Pilgrim's Progress' (Fisher, Reid)
It's curious to go from a song called 'Crucifiction Lane' to one with a title that positively references the quest for redemption through faith. Again, that's the only link – the lyric is Reid scrutinising himself once more and coming up short, this time as a writer. It chronicles the beginning of what he later

admitted was a period in which lyrics came to him slowly and with difficulty, even though this period also corresponds with the triumph of *Home*. Two more nautical references ('anchor', 'pirate's gold') round off the album neatly. But the most telling line is the last, an admission that for Reid, the process of writing was one of adapting other people's words and passing them on for other people to adapt in turn: much the same approach that Brooker took with music.

Fisher had become one of the dominant voices in Procol Harum, both as a player, writer, and even singer, and here he gets a last hurrah as a member of the original group. The mesmeric, fugal sound is his, and he plays almost all the instruments. Though his voice is thin and required double-tracking, its Bee Gees-style plaintiveness suits the piece. There's also a lovely coda, which adds a little curlicue to the end of *A Salty Dog* just as 'Grand Finale' did for *Shine On Brightly*. *Crawdaddy* quoted Fisher in 1969: 'I couldn't for the life of me think of a way to end it except for the very obvious way, which would have been to go back to the beginning bit. That would have been anticlimactic. Even before I finished writing the song, I had that sort of closing bit in mind for the end. It may look as if it were stuck on as an afterthought, but it wasn't'.

The return of Fisher's Hammond as the dominant tone was just as notable (we would surely miss that in the future) as is the fact that 'Pilgrim's Progress' is one of the few Procol Harum songs with a contrasting middle section. It's this section that Fisher adapted for his coda, accented by a tubular bell that is presumably intended to be the tolling of a ship's bell, accompanying the aural equivalent of the band's ship heading cinematically away.

'Long Gone Geek' (Brooker, Fisher, Reid)
Whether this song is evidence of Reid's incipient writer's block or merely because the band needed a song – *any* song – to throw on the B-side to 'A Salty Dog', this track rightfully had no place on the parent album. Its words were old and rejected – as much as two years out of date and from a quite different and more-primitive style than the current band. The title is another link back to Dylan's 'Ballad Of A Thin Man', while the lyric is reminiscent of all Reid's early attempts at Americana squashed shapelessly together. We hear about the various inmates of an American jail, including a cowardly sheriff, Pinstriped Sweet (familiar from an aside at the end of 'Lime Street Blues') and his gun-carrying cat, and the titular hardcase Geek who bursts in rootin' for revenge. The song is played boisterously as riff-driven heavy rock, and Brooker sings with his customary sincerity, but it's more than the lyric deserves. The song was never likely to become a band classic, though it was a dependable live feature.

Home (1970)

Personnel:
Gary Brooker: piano, accordion, double bass, vocals
Chris Copping: bass, organ
Robin Trower: guitars
B.J. Wilson: drums
Harry Pitch: harmonica ('Your Own Choice')
Ealing Technical College Choir: vocals ('Whaling Stories')
Recorded: February 1970, EMI Studios, London, UK
Producer: Chris Thomas
Label: Regal Zonophone
Release date: June 1970
Charts: UK: 49, US: 34
Running time: 39:01 (A: 21:16, B: 17:45)

Grim days beget grim songs, and this album contains some of the grimmest
ever written. It begins with an alcoholic's last hopeless vow to straighten
out, shifts inexorably through destitution, bereavement, sacrifice, flattened
chances, divine genocide, and wasted struggle, and ends with suicide. The
lightest song is about a bloody vendetta.

Home isn't nearly as much fun as its cover suggests.

It's also the height of Procol Harum's power, their most realised and singular
sound world, the fiercest flowering of their obsessions, and the culmination of
the ambitions that Brooker and Reid had built for themselves little more than
three giddy years earlier. Here, the gothic darkness of *Shine On Brightly* and
the wider vistas opened by *A Salty Dog* are merged, at last and satisfyingly.
There are no weak moments, no songs you'd choose to skip. How could you,
when the point of *Home* (among other things, the title means death) is that
every move you make is fated and unfair? Each square along the game of
Snakes and Ladders, which is a metaphor for life, is loaded against you. There
are no ladders on the cover, only snakes. You take these lumps one after
another dutifully, as is your due. That board game was originally intended as
a morality-teaching device for children. On *Home*, it teaches that every step
leads to the grave. Dickinson's tatty collage – in which you can even see some
turned-up edges – was built partly out of characters snipped from copies of
The Beano (itself barely disguised morality tales for schoolkids) and juxtaposes
Brooker (as Biffo the Bear) jumping into a bucket of water with nuclear
armageddon. A Superman-type figure provides the only ascension, carrying a
smug-looking Trower to Heaven. It was hardly as powerful a sleeve as either
of its predecessors, but it did disguise an unfamiliar face in the lineup, and
also that Procol Harum had shrunk in number.

Much more compelling is the inner photo by David Bailey, in which
a narrow-eyed Brooker forcefully enunciates some point of fact to Reid,
jabbing his finger straight out at the viewer while the rest of the band

cowers beneath. Wilson's reaction (being Wilson) is a yawn. The interloper is new bassist Chris Copping, meaning that what we witness in that photo and on the disc is a performing band consisting entirely of members of The Paramounts, even though Copping left that group way back in 1963 and had never actually been in the same lineup as Wilson. What goes around comes around, and the cover and title also signified that by all the vagaries of chance and ill fortune, The Paramounts had somehow found themselves home.

We can't *quite* be sure of cause and effect in the music. Reid's bleakest-ever set of words saw him struggling to make his breakthrough as an artist, given a scene that was now not just crowded with singer-songwriters but with other non-performing lyricists/poets like Bernie Taupin, Pete Sinfield, and Robert Hunter. Reid's hook was rank corpses and creaking coffins on the sea, which had begun to verge on parody (like 'Pale' but even more twisted), and this was one of the reasons Fisher wanted out. Reid moaned to *Hit Parader* in 1972 that he was just being a realist: 'I don't believe anybody is a happy person. I've never met anybody who is a happy person. Being alive is not a happy experience'.

The toughening of the band's sound on *Home* may have been a reaction to the darkening words. But with Fisher's departure, the others were forced to abandon the Hammond that had added a church-like richness to their sound. It was a return to The Paramounts in more ways than one: it was more R&B-based, more raw, and with more space for Trower. Reid explained to *Zigzag* in 1973:

> When Matthew left, we decided that we wouldn't get another organist but would be a four-piece group, with the bass player playing organ on certain numbers. From that point on, we stopped featuring the organ as strongly as we had, and consequently, the guitar came out more. Robin began to play a more dominant part in the group sound and naturally began to want to contribute more to the songwriting side of things, too, so by the time we came to make the Home album, he had written the music for two of the songs.

In fact, Trower had contributed to *three* songs on *A Salty Dog*, but Reid's basic flow is still correct. The de-emphasis on Hammond *did* give Trower more scope to play, as long as the song was a blues. Most importantly, unlike much of *A Salty Dog*, the album was in a style that could be reproduced live on stage: a new body of songs built with post-Fisher performance in mind. More bluesy indeed, by design.

But the live work was a struggle. As a four-piece, Copping was forced to hop between bass and organ. If a song could be arranged to work without guitar, Trower was obliged to switch to bass. When all else failed, Copping played both the bass part and organ lines on his manuals (as opposed to organ foot pedals). Reid even sat in on organ at least once.

As now seemed to be the band's custom, the entire early sessions for the album at Trident Studios were scrapped when the band fell out irrevocably with Fisher, who was slated to produce the album. Work began again at Abbey Road with inexperienced producer Chris Thomas, recommended to the band by George Martin. Thomas struggled to constrain the band's force. The mix wasn't quite as crisp as *A Salty Dog*, tending toward the same kind of brutalist thumping that Regal Zonophone labelmates The Move were fashioning for their *Looking On* album that year.

'Whisky Train' (Trower, Reid)

Chris Thomas had a great idea when the band rolled into Abbey Road to begin work on the new album. Since they weren't making much money, and since they'd honed themselves into a tight and powerful stage act, why not record the album live to two-track tape? This meant the whole thing would be quick and cheap and would retain all the excitement of the band roaring through songs in the flesh. Though the released working tapes from earlier albums show that the band *did* overdub, for the *Home* sessions, they had an ease and familiarity with each other that was demonstrated by their habit of starting each day's session by playing old R&B songs to exercise the fingers. Thomas must have reasoned that if they could do *those* songs live, they could do the album the same way.

He loaded up the two-track on the first night and hit record on a sole, terrific take of 'Whisky Train' – Trower alternating a stinging riff and snarling solos, Brooker and Copping piling in with a tarmac-skimming rhythm, and Wilson slapping merrily at the cowbell in between fills of John Bonham ferocity. Above it all, Brooker lays down a note-perfect vocal in which he seems to live every word of Reid's desperate lyric about a man determined that this time, *this* time, he's giving up the bottle for good.

And you know what? Thomas was right. 'Whisky Train' is an album highlight, the perfect high-wattage opener, the hands-down best candidate for a single (though, with dreary predictability, it wasn't a hit), and the most coruscating the band had sounded in ages. They could have done the whole album this way. Unlike *A Salty Dog*, it's a stripped-down affair with no orchestra and is almost entirely lacking in forays to that instrument cupboard under the stairs. It might well have turned out *even better*. But when the band realised what their producer was up to, they immediately leaned on him to go back to multi-tracking, and consequently, it very much seems like all their energies were channelled not into the album itself but into those R&B rave-ups. A shame.

'The Dead Man's Dream' (Brooker, Reid)

It's hard to think of a greater contrast than this – from the band's fiercest all-out rocker to date to its most static and funereal mood piece. Reid claimed an unlikely inspiration, as he explained to *Creem* in 1972: 'I saw *Midnight Cowboy*, and that affected me quite a lot, and I wrote that song after I'd seen it. It doesn't have anything to do with the film *Midnight Cowboy*, but with the way that film made me feel'.

You can understand why a movie about down-and-outs in New York would appeal to Reid (they're urban sailors in his mythology). And though the movie *does* end with a death, it's not quite as grim as the song that resulted. A dying man – apparently homeless, given that his deathbed is the floor and 'a bundle of newspaper' serves as his pillow – experiences a vision of a city cemetery full of opened coffins with decaying, maggot-ridden corpses. He screams, awakens, and dies, with the final words 'I slithered under' suggesting that what he's witnessed is a vision of Hell and that that's just where he's headed.

Musically, it feels like a conscious recap of the themes of 'In Held 'Twas In I', including Brooker's mournful piano, Copping's phantom organ counterpoint, and leaden-footed band eruptions driven by Wilson's momentous fills. There's even a recitation. The piece ends with an 'A Day In The Life'-style piano chord left to decay for 26 seconds before a great rumbling coda sounds out like the stones of a mausoleum rattling back into place. It's effective for sure and something of a highlight, but it's not for the unwary.

'Still There'll Be More' (Brooker, Reid)

If 'The Dead Man's Dream' wants you down in the deep, 'Still There'll Be More' wants you up and kicking over other people's dustbins. Like Dylan, Reid weaponises his lyric, seeing public song as the ultimate means of revenge on an enemy: you can say what you like, and no comeback is possible. Of course, there's a difference between 'Like A Rolling Stone' – which cruelly imagines its hapless female victim as a destitute tramp turning tricks in back alleys – and 'Still There'll Be More', which merely wants to do unspeakable things on the victim's doorstep. If Dylan jabs with a pin, Reid blusters around with a bag full of poop. What makes the song so delicious is that it's an achievable revenge. You can't actually *think* somebody into the gutter, but you sure can sneak over and vandalise their garden.

The lyric is one of Reid's best. No longer is he a weedy, spectacled loser. Now he's a marauding colossus who divests himself of tears in the first line and sets about laying waste to his victim's world in the rest – uprooting his trees, blighting his crops, and – in the most savage couplet – abducting, raping, and blinding his wife and daughter. But the most glee is in Reid's one moment of Procol Harum transgression. 'I'll blacken your Christmas and piss on your door', he promises. The image is no less startling for being so petty: you're an Old Testament God, big as the sky, and *this* is the worst you can think up? Brooker obviously thought the words were a hoot as he matched them to a galloping rhythm and an irresistible sing-along melody.

'Nothing That I Didn't Know' (Brooker, Reid)

This aching lament for a dead woman is one of the band's most affecting ballads. Reid told *Creem* in 1972: 'I saw a play which was about that situation, and then I kind of wrote a song which just retold the story. So that was a pretty straightforward song'.

The cause of Jenny's death is not revealed here, only that she grew thin and pale (a word sung with the utmost gravity) and was finally released from her suffering. Reid's reaction, 'I wish that I could have died instead', lends the song a harrowing empathy, especially when sung with Brooker's sincerity. It deflates the glee of 'Still There'll Be More' and sets up the anger of 'About To Die' – a picked scab at the heart of the album. Sonically, the outstanding features are Copping's organ solo and Brooker's touches of Gallic accordion.

'About To Die' (Trower, Reid)

Reid's most savage lyric on *Home* was written from the perspective of a Christian hauled out for public execution in a Roman coliseum. While he cannot escape his death, he's nevertheless secure in his resurrection since 'the saviour's son' is soon sure to destroy his enemies. The pun on 'son' as a source of light is negated by the utter darkness in which the song is performed. Trower's knotty Leslie-treated guitar riff forms the aural centre around which the others cluster, but Brooker's piano takes the solos and offers no chance of transcendence.

'Barnyard Story' (Brooker, Reid)

Just as side two of *A Salty Dog* started with a Trower feature, so does side two of *Home* begin with a relatively unadorned piano/vocal feature for Brooker. The only additions are Copping's funereal organ drone and Brooker on double bass.

'Barnyard Story' contains Procol Harum's most famous misheard line: 'Once I stood upon a lamppost'. That's the way I heard it for years, even though the correct words were right there on the lyric sheet (or inner gatefold in the US), and it's how I *still* hear it unless I tell myself otherwise. Chris Thomas heard it that way, too, and questioned Brooker about it in the studio, only for Reid to lean ominously out of the shadows to correct him. The word is 'Olympus', but it hardly changes the meaning. It's still a man who thought himself tall, realising he's just a grub in the dirt. The rest of the lyric is a mash of *non sequitur*s and Reid clichés, culminating in what's either the first of the album side's declarations of suicide or the promise that death will – thankfully – finally shut up that infernal voice in our heads.

'Piggy Pig Pig' (Brooker, Reid)

If the brief swerve into the farmyard for the first two lines of the previous song was perplexing, what can we make of *this* title? (And what did Reid *expect* to call the song?) It was chosen in response to Brooker's use of the phrase to demonstrate the rhythm to the others. An alternate mix reveals that Brooker accompanied himself with improvised snorting noises and chanting from the start of the song, and not just at the end as we hear it on the album.

Above: The Procol Harum line-up in 1967. From left to right: Ray Royer, Matthew Fisher, Gary Brooker, Dave Knights, Bobby Harrison. (*Tony Gale*)

Below: The band in 1970 posing at the Amsterdam Hilton Hotel, Netherlands. From left to right: Chris Copping, Gary Brooker, B.J. Wilson, Keith Reid, Robin Trower. (*Gijsbert Hanekroot/Redferns*)

DOLENZ: take-off

in September.
There is now a possibility
that the Monkees will ar-
rive in Britain on June 28—
two days before they start

Procol Harum single roars into chart

THE Procol Harum roared
into the Pop 30 at num-
ber 14 this week with " A
Whiter Shade of Pale,"
Decca's fastest selling British group single to date.

The group guests in Top
Of The Pops tonight (Thurs-
day), Dee Time (June 1), Pop
North (June 5) and Monday,
Monday (12).

They make their concert
debut at London's Saville Theatre on June 4, on a bill with
the Jimi Hendrix Experience
and Denny Laine.

● TEDDY WILSON

WILSON OPENS

AMERICAN piano star
Teddy Wilson opens his
British tour with the Dave
Shepherd quintet at Osterley
Jazz Club on Friday (June 2).

"Paper Sun" tipped for the
top by pop critics, is due for
release next Friday.

"We are just not doing
any appearances until later
in the year," Stevie told the
MM on Monday. "This is deliberate because most groups
get themselves worked in on
the road first, and we won't be
able to do that. We have to
make a good impression right
away, so we shall be spending
some time rehearsing at home
during the summer.

EUROPEAN HOLIDAY

THE Beach Boys' European
tour ended in Berlin on
Sunday and the group split
for separate holidays in
Europe.

(9), Hampstead (12) and Purcell Room (13), Hitchin (14),
London's Purcell Room (15)
and Manchester (18).

TRAFFIC HOLD UP

STEV

VAUDE

THE Ne
were
North Pole
day (We
weeks cal
Tropicana
They fl
route to L
on to La
America,
appear on
coast pro
Lead vo
the MM:
arrive in
to see th
show for
appearance

MORE

THE tw
Benne
certs put
Hammers
Sunday, J
many fans
getting t
shows hav
sold out.
But two
formances
CADS, h
for the Bla
for Tuesda

Above: The first the world
knew of Procol Harum
was a small announcement
inside *Melody Maker* on 27
May 1967 ...

Right: ... and this
more substantial piece
in *Disc And Music
Echo* the same day.
Both band and smash
hit 'A Whiter Shade
Of Pale' appeared
out of nowhere, with
zero live work or
publicity beforehand.

PROCOL HARUM: cats with Bach and bite

ONCE in a while, among the vast piles of singles that swamp
Disc's offices every week, there appears a record that sends
everyone in sight into wild uncontrollable ecstasies of delight.

The record is the weirdly-titled "A Whiter Shade Of Pale,"
by the weirdly-named Procol Harum.

Sounding like a cross between a church cantata and a Bach
fugue, the record is stimulating enormous interest. So much so,
that the group, formed only two months ago, have been signed to
the Harold Davison Organisation and can now look forward to a
very rosy future.

The thought behind Procol Harum (the name came from a
pedigree Persian cat) is lead singer and pianist Gary Brooker,
formerly lead singer with the Paramounts.

Gary had sounds going through his head, and decided to gather
a few friends together just for the fun of it.

Record producer Denny Cordell heard the sounds, raved, and
"A Whiter Shade Of Pale" was born.

The outstanding organ on the record comes from ex-Guildhall
School of Music student, Mathew Fisher.

Mathew only recently completed his music studies, and the clever
blending of classical patterns into a pop record are proof indeed
that his studies were not wasted.

The other members of Procol Harum are Ray Royer (lead
guitar), Dave Knight (bass guitar) and Bobby Harrison (drums)—
and the average age of the group is nearly 22.

"We don't believe in saying we are younger than we are, like so
many groups," they say.

Sales of "A Whiter Shade Of Pale" are little short of astrono-
mical. Last week alone the record sold 90,000 copies, of which
27,000 were in one day.

And all this with virtually no live performances.

But now the doors have opened and Procol Harum are all ready
for the key programmes. They are set to appear in "Top Of The
Pops" tonight (Thursday), "Dee Time" next Thursday, and "As
You Like It" on June 6.

On live performances they are guaranteeing the same type of
music—and a very new sound. It will be worth waiting for.

H
c
t

BRIT
popu
frenz
Hend
ute in
them.
So
Mitch
unsus
No
bass
small
of he
Jimi
Mitch
clothe
bury.
plaine
Germ
off h
W
hotel
partic
they c
I thin
"A
all th
street
They
so far
a bo
matte
The
a few
at
birthp
they
the H
as th
alread

WHERE IT'S AT

Right: By 10 June, the song had roared to the top of the charts and Procol Harum were arrayed across the covers of all the British weeklies.

Left: From nothing to triumph to disaster in the space of seven feverish weeks. The single was still number one when Procol Harum's world came crashing down on the front of *Melody Maker* on 15 July.

Left: 'A Whiter Shade Of Pale', released in this unassuming generic sleeve, remains one of the best-loved singles of all time. (*Deram*)

Right: In America, a well-timed first album rode the single's success. At home, it wasn't released until December, long after any remaining interest had waned. (*Deram*)

Left: Second single 'Homburg' is just as extraordinary as the first. This is the German picture sleeve. (*Polydor*)

Above: Procol Harum announced 'Homburg' with adverts in the British weeklies at the end of September 1967. The band's name treatment would be the closest Procol Harum ever came to an official logo.

Right: 'Homburg' also saw a brief dalliance with cosmic troubadour costumes by The Fool, actually cast-offs that The Move had refused to wear. Left to right: Matthew Fisher, Robin Trower, B.J. Wilson (front), Dave Knights, Gary Brooker.

Left and below: While the band floundered in Britain, America adored them. Here, they're immortalised in some of San Francisco's most iconic posters.

Right: The American release of second album *Shine On Brightly* came in a cover that matched the disk's unsettling, haunted mystery... (*A&M*)

Left: ...while the British cover by painter George Underwood positions the band as a piece with The Moody Blues. (*Regal Zonophone*)

Right: The 1968 single 'Il Tuo Diamante' was the title track with new words in Italian. (*IL*)

Left: Designer Dickinson's striking cover for *A Salty Dog*. From now on, 'hero' Keith Reid would be as much a feature of the band's covers as any performing member. (*A&M/ Regal Zonophone*)

Below: Dickinson's wraparound snakes-and-ladders collage for *Home* might have been a game you could play, except it was poorly realised, and in the UK, it didn't even come in a gatefold cover. (*A&M/Regal Zonophone*)

Left: 'Oi, Reid. Enough of the bloody corpses, all right?' *Home*'s superb inner photo surely should have been the cover. Left to right: Reid, Trower, Wilson, Chris Copping, Brooker. (*David Bailey*)

Right: The die-cut cover for *Broken Barricades* finally showed the band on the front. (*A&M/Chrysalis*)

Left: *Procol Harum Live* was an attractively packaged album and an unexpected triumph. (*A&M/ Chrysalis*)

Right: The kick that *Procol Harum Live* gave the band was not followed through to the studio. The cover of *Grand Hotel* aimed for old-world elegance but looks cold and fussy. (*Chrysalis*)

Left: Gary Brooker, the voice and soul of Procol Harum, at the ivories in 1976. (*Gijsbert Hanekroot*)

Above: Mick Grabham and Chris Copping at the Bilzen festival in August 1973. Procol Harum headlined on the second day. (*Gijsbert Hanekroot*)

Right: Procol Harum's performance for *Rockpalast* at WDR Studio, Cologne in 1976 saw the band at the peak of their powers. Brooker ...

Left: ... Grabham, Copping and Cartwright.

Below: 'The waiter brought a tray'. Keith Reid dishes up the performing band on the inner spread of *Grand Hotel*. Left to right: Brooker, Mick Grabham's head on Dave Ball's body, Copping, Wilson, Cartwright. (*Jeffrey Weisel*)

Left: Sumptuous lettering and colours and a striking 17th-century painting by Jakob Bogdani make *Exotic Birds And Fruit* the best-looking Procol Harum album of all. (*Chrysalis*)

Right: Was the cover of *Exotic Birds And Fruit* too distancing? Procol Harum crashed back to personal connection with the punningly-titled *Procol's Ninth*. (*Chrysalis*)

Left: France-only single 'The Adagio D'Albinoni' was surely never going to tickle the charts, particularly when, once again, only Wilson could summon up a smile. (*Chrysalis*)

Right: The *Something Magic* cover painting by *Procol Harum Live* artist Bruce Meek suggested a little of the old surrealism but also gave the unfortunate impression that the band were now headless. (*Chrysalis*)

Left: Brooker revived Procol Harum in 1991, pulling in Reid, Fisher and Trower for this late-career shot at the big time. *The Prodigal Stranger* is a better disk than the wintry, faceless cover suggests. (*Zoo Entertainment*)

Right: From rain to fire. The whirling computer-style cover to second studio resurrection *The Well's On Fire* tried hard to be contemporary. (*Eagle Records*)

Left: For her *Novum* cover, artist Julia Brown subtly reinvented Procol Harum's past while sprinkling a little hopeful star shine on their future. (*Eagle Records*)

Right: Procol Harum bowed out with this overlooked CD single in 2021, now forever to take its place as an apparent last-minute reconciliation between Brooker and Reid, even though it wasn't. (*Esoteric Antenna*)

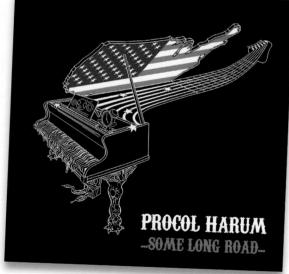

Left: *Some Long Road* is a live album containing performances from the band's 2012 and 2013 tours of Europe and the US. (*Union Square Records*)

Right: Released as part of Record Store Day 'Black Friday' in 2017, *The One And Only One* is a 10" live EP containing four tracks from the band's first few gigs in 2017. (*Eagle Records*)

Left: There's a bewildering array of Procol Harum compilations. Of special note to collectors are these two box sets, which mix studio and live recordings: *All This And More* was released in 2009. (*Salvo*)

Right: And here is the 2018 5-CD, 3-DVD set *Still There'll Be More,* the most sumptuous overview to date. (*Esoteric Recordings*)

LAST WEEK A POEM MADE NO. 11 IN ENGLAND FIRST WEEK OF RELEASE

we skipped the light fandango
and turned cartwheels cross the floor
I was feeling kind of seasick
but the crowd called out for more
the room was humming harder
as the ceiling flew away
when we called out for another drink
the waiter brought a tray
and so it was that later
as the Miller told his tale
that her face at first just ghostly
turned a whiter shade of pale

she said "i'm home on shore leave"
(though in truth we were at sea)
so I took her by the looking glass
and forced her to agree
saying "you must be the mermaid
who took Neptune for a ride"
but she smiled at me so sadly
that my anger straightway died
and so it was that later
as the Miller told his tale
that her face at first just ghostly
turned a whiter shade of pale

she said "there is no reason
and the truth is plain to see"
but I wandered through my playing cards
and would not let her be
one of sixteen vestal virgins
who were leaving for the coast
and although my eyes were open
they might have just as well been closed
and so it was that later
as the Miller told his tale
that her face at first just ghostly
turned a whiter shade of pale

KEITH REID - By Permission

SET TO MUSIC BY PROCOL HARUM YOU HAVE "A WHITER SHADE OF PALE"
(THIS WEEK IT'S NO. 3)

#7507

DERAM
A PRODUCT OF
London

PRODUCED BY DENNY CORDELL FOR NEW BREED PRODUCTIONS

Left: In June 1967, Deram introduced 'A Whiter Shade Of Pale' to America with a full-page ad in *Billboard* that highlighted its lyrics, including Keith Reid's unrecorded second verse.

Right: Half a century later, it's still just as beloved. Here's the cover of the *50th Anniversary* EP version, complete with vintage logo. (*Fly Records*)

Reid's lyric is another evocation of the bellowing, monstrous Old Testament God, one under which the inhabitants of a seemingly medieval town scurry around with heads bent. Like much of the imagery on *Home*, life is presented merely as a graveyard in waiting. Here, the streets are 'awash with blood and pus', but the song also contains some of Reid's most powerful lines. 'Counting houses full of lead' is not just a clever inversion; it's a nightmare anticipation of our own times when mass shootings have become too commonplace to make headlines. The band match the words with one of the album's most compelling performances: an unrelenting tongue-tied rhythm to which Trower adds squalls of guitar.

'Whaling Stories' (Brooker, Reid)

In a year in which side-length tracks had become rock currency, 'Whaling Stories' isn't much of an epic at just seven minutes in length. Nevertheless, it's the band's longest single studio piece (that is, one not divided into sections) from the vinyl years and is beaten only by 'Can't Say That' on *Novum*, which is ten seconds longer. But Brooker did wonders with the piece. The lyric is just 16 lines long, consisting of four verses, with the same leisurely 4/4 meter throughout, and it's to Brooker's eternal credit that he made each verse sound quite different to the others, even though you can easily interchange the words between them. For the first time, a Procol Harum song has a symphonic-like structure, as opposed to the simple contrasts of 'Repent Walpurgis' or the patch-and-hope construction of 'In Held 'Twas In I'. There's a quiet stretch, a loud stretch, a lull, and the triumphal finish. The result is a piece that sounds unified even though it has nothing resembling a chorus and boasts a satisfying, elegant shape that would soon become standard among the many prog-rock bands that followed its example. Trower plays a career-high solo, and the choral ending is exhilarating.

What it *means*? Well, that's a different matter. The title suggests it's a holdover from *A Salty Dog*: another nautical voyage to uncharted parts, related by the humbled survivor. But that's not quite what we hear. 'Whaling Stories' gains gravitas and distancing from its repeated use of the passive tense – 'a mammoth task was set', 'rum was served' – that seems to purposefully avoid the need to mention a narrator. There's no I, no we. There's not even a ship or a whale, though we do get references to sailors, rum, six bells, and more. According to the printed lyric, the first word is 'pailing': possibly a pun that merges 'pail' or (dare I say it) 'pale' with 'bailing'. For what it's worth, it sounds to me like Brooker sings 'bailing'.

But we're also in a town, a movie, or heaven. The wordplay suggests somewhere of dreamy seaside isolation, like Dylan Thomas's Llareggub. There's a storm, which also seems oddly cinematic ('flashbulbs glorified the scene'), and in the aftermath, the settlement picks itself up to the sparkling of a new day and goes off to count its dead. With equal degrees of unlikeliness for a man who claimed he hadn't read Chaucer or Milton, the perplexing cry of 'Shalimar!' evokes the divine cries of the thunder in T. S. Eliot's *The Waste Land* and the use of the word in Amy Woodforde-Finden's poem 'Kashmiri Song', which also begins with the word 'pale'. Less in doubt is the beauty of Reid's final line, in which 'wake' refers to the mourning of the deceased, the turbulent water left by a ship, and the totting-up of the good and evil we did in our lives.

'Your Own Choice' (Brooker, Reid)
Nothing could ever follow the majesty of 'Whaling Stories', but 'Your Own Choice' makes a strong case for being the album's most attractive song. Just as 'Still There'll Be More' began with a count-in to remind us that this is a band playing live, so does 'Your Own Choice' narrow us back to the specifics of the recording session: there's a false start when Trower checks his gear over the top of it.

The tune is one of Brooker's prettiest, and the track has a pleasing grandeur that doesn't try to compete with its more showy predecessor. There's also a surprise in the closing seconds – virtuoso Harry Pitch plays a harmonica solo, an instrument the band had previously only used prominently on 'Juicy John Pink'. It all adds up to Procol Harum's most perfect three minutes.

It was the ideal single to revive their fortunes, you'd think. But the lyric's sequence of homey pulpitry is simultaneously one of Reid's sneakiest instances of self-analysis and one of his most distressing proclamations on the human condition. He tells us there are no solutions to the problems of life except to throw yourself in a river. In an age when rock was being accused of all kinds of demonic influence on young people, the title alone would have had moralists fuming.

Broken Barricades (1971)

Personnel:
Gary Brooker: piano, vocals
Chris Copping: bass, organ
Robin Trower: guitar, vocals
B.J. Wilson: drums
Chris Thomas: Moog
Recorded: December 1970-March 1971, AIR Studios, London, UK
Producer: Chris Thomas
Label: Chrysalis
Release date: April 1971 (US), June 1971 (UK)
Charts: US: 32, UK: 42
Running time: 35:01 (A: 16:36, B: 18:25)

The second and last album with the Paramounts lineup feels like an anomaly in the band's catalogue. It's an abrupt shift in direction that acts as a mental bump in the road before things return to relatively smooth running for the second half of the original band's career. For one thing, the album lacks any Hammond organ swells, a deliberate cold-shouldering of the old sound. But it's also short on songs and short on ideas.

It's an awkward place to bow out on Trower, whose departure had seemed increasingly likely in an era of superstar guitarists. Though his fierce phrasing had been a band feature from the start, and though his vocals weren't distinguished, he saw around him other blues players with no better chops who were either solo performers or the undisputed star of their respective bands. Trower could play and he could write. The Procol Harum style was now a constriction. Reid told *Zigzag* in 1973: 'When we came to make the *Broken Barricades* album – which really he wrote half the music for – it was obvious that he would have to go and form his own group. It was just a natural progression due to circumstances in that Matthew left and then we were a four-piece. Robin was called on to do more, he eventually *did* do more, and eventually reached the stage where he wanted to do the whole thing'.

Brooker told *Prog* in 2018: 'He was always a great guitarist, but he had to invent a different way of playing for the music that I'd written for Procol's first, second and third albums. It wasn't an easy twang-along. The easy part of it was that he had to play a blues solo and it sounded right. But when he couldn't figure out the chord – or if it's in E flat, which guitarists don't like – he would just find a good low guitar note that would vibrate through it all'.

It's easy to understand why this happened. Electric guitarists generally learn their instrument by playing folk or rock in some form. Pianists learn from classical tutors. Being piano-based, much of the band's music was alien to an instinctive blues guitarist like Trower. He could abide the more difficult pieces only if there were chances to kick back and solo. Now, he'd gained at least a modicum of audience recognition; it was better to ditch the more difficult pieces altogether and play blues changes all night. Trower told *Rolling Stone* in 1973: "Song For A Dreamer' was the first song where I had done it all. I sang it, I wrote it, I played just about everything on it. It was the first time I realised that I could do something. After that, there was no question that I had to go out on my own'. He meant the song was a distinctive Trower vision rather than just something he'd played all by himself. He still needed a *band* to perform with.

The album cover – the first without a bold illustration – signalled a different way of presenting the group. My suspicion is that the die-cut front flap was meant to illustrate the album title: here are the holes in our defences, through which the members themselves are revealed for the first time, without artifice, a group of performers onstage. The disc itself was the ultimate defence, pulled out of an internal pocket arranged like a castle keep. But it didn't work. It wasn't well-designed, the holes didn't open to reveal anything astounding, and there was no sense of occasion or flavour that made you leap to pluck it from the rack. The portrait of Reid on the back was better, but Reid had defences of his own. For example, there were lyrics on the cardboard, but like on *Home,* Reid chose to show only some of them.

Regarding the four that *were* presented, an awkward fact emerges – three were in exactly the same plodding 4/4 time. The mundane meter reflected the words, which had become trite and earthy. 'Song For A Dreamer' leaps out as a treasure buried in an otherwise blockheaded side two. Remove that track and the album is immeasurably poorer.

If Reid was stumbling, even more was Brooker, who provided the double punch of the album's standout opening tracks but then essentially coasted on empty for the rest. There were more Trower songs because the space needed to be filled. There were certainly no grand gestures like 'Whaling Stories', though even with their simplified approach, the band would have been capable of performing them live. Brooker later expressed his dislike of the 'Luskus Delph' lyric, but the obvious question is why he chose to put it to music. He admitted to *Street Life* in 1976 that this was not an easy album for him to make: '*Broken Barricades* was written in the studio mostly, and therefore somewhat haphazard. But there were financial considerations as well. We hadn't made a great deal of money, and what with people deciding – reasonably enough – that they weren't prepared to carry on regardless, well, as you can imagine, we didn't feel on top of the world'. He was implying that the loss of Fisher still haunted him, and *Broken Barricades* was a blind groping forward from a band that had been battered almost into oblivion, had made no commercial breakthrough since 1967, and were now in the worst pits of their self-doubt. Among other problems, Wilson was showing visible signs of stress and had begun drinking heavily. The back cover credit to tape operator Chris Michie for 'comic relief' was pointed. With his high spirits, Michie contributed much more than simply winding the tape backwards and forwards.

There was reason to be optimistic. The band had a new contract with Chrysalis – one of the hippest labels in Britain – which saw the usual advance-recouping promotional push and, at long last, some serious press attention in their home country. But Trower's departure put the all-important touring on hold and meant yet another round of dispiriting auditions. There would be no album of new songs in 1972, and indeed, it's unclear if Brooker and Reid made any concerted effort to write *at all* between the early 1971 *Broken Barricades* sessions and those for *Grand Hotel* almost two years and a whole lot more churn later.

'Simple Sister' (Brooker, Reid)
This is a vicious lyric, even by Reid's standards. Assuming there's no hidden meaning (and Reid never hinted that there was), what we have is a grim Victorian children's story of the hair-pulling, cat-drowning variety. The sister of the title is not only mentally disabled, she's suffering from a contagious disease, and the lyric describes the delight with which her sibling (evidently also a girl) tells her all the ways her life is going to be made worse as a result, presumably hollered through a closed door. Some make sense, such as burning her toys to prevent infection. Others are mere spite.

Brooker set this to the band's heaviest guitar riff, written to feature Trower and give him a means of becoming a guitar hero while still in the band. We could be *your* band, Brooker is suggesting. But the effect is tempered by an arrangement that seemed to run away with itself into such flights of fancy that you may not even notice that Trower plays one of his most dazzling solos: banks of piano multitracked at different tape speeds, and a marvellous baroque orchestral arrangement from George Martin, who conducts it with all the gusto of his days when working with The Beatles was stimulating and fun. You might have thought Brooker was exactly what Martin wanted at this time: a man of classical abilities like Paul McCartney but more sophisticated and demanding. Together, Martin and Brooker could have taken both their crafts to greater heights.

For the hair-raising central section, Brooker lifted the bass rhythm almost verbatim from The Capitols' 1966 hit 'Cool Jerk' and built it into a triumphant crescendo. The result is almost six minutes of some of the band's best music and their most powerful opener to that date. There was rightly a single, and guess what it did?

'Broken Barricades' (Brooker, Reid)
As great as 'Simple Sister' is, 'Broken Barricades' is the album standout thanks to another fine lyric and Brooker's even more elaborate treatment. Reid seems to have had the degradation of the environment in mind, mixed with his usual Biblical apocalypse, which stirs in abandoned temples and dead children. We are also returned to the 'Conquistador' image of the fallen warrior, vanquished now by the vengeance of the dying world: 'The seaweed and the cobweb have rotted your sword'.

Brooker's job was harder for this song. It could have been another roar of anger or another lament. But he chose a middle ground, thickening his waltz-time piano riff with carefully shadowing electric guitars and a bright but synthetic Moog operated by an uncredited Chris Thomas, evoking the aural equivalent of a sea awash in plastic waste.

'Memorial Drive' (Trower, Reid)

This blistering song is steered fully by Trower, which means it is stripped-down heavy blues without any orchestra or synthesizer. The band pile on manfully, but Brooker's voice isn't quite suited to this style. Trower's thinner, uglier tone might have worked better. An extended ending gives the band time to rock out, but Trower isn't interested in soloing and simply rides the riff.

Reid's densely allusive text tells the grievous story of a 'Zulu queen' sold into slavery in the US and 'worked like a Mexican donkey'. The line 'used like a hole in the ground' suggests not just that she's shat upon but that she's also debased sexually. The horror of this fate is in contrast with the woman's inner radiance, the true value of which her white owners never realise or – just as likely – don't care to know. The most potent image is of the woman's wish to 'drink the whole ocean dry' in order to fuel her tears and give her the means to walk home. It's a shame about the title, though, which is merely a pun on 'slave driver'.

'Luskus Delph' (Brooker, Reid)

'An obscene song', Brooker told *New Musical Express* in 1971. 'The treatment of it should be banned'. But before you think it's all booty-shaking and grunting noises, 1971 was a world away from the porn-pop business we live with now. Reid delighted in juvenile imagery that veered just close enough to the literary that even the BBC might have been taken in by 'tulip lips', 'peach preserve', 'widow's crack' or 'Turkish pearl'. They sure wouldn't have been fooled by 'The inside sweetness of your cave' or 'Shove me in your steaming vat'. Brooker never tired of telling audiences that 'Luskus' evokes 'lust' and 'suck'. But the song sure must have confused the inhabitants of Delph in Manchester.

Delightfully, Brooker's reaction to the words wasn't boudoir Hammond organ but his sweetest orchestral arrangement, turning what could have been tossed-off prurience into another triumph.

'Power Failure' (Brooker, Reid)

At the time, any band faced the ordeal of a sudden power loss on stage, leaving just the unamplified drums to project into the hall. Procol Harum were no exception, as Brooker told *New Musical Express* in 1971: 'It's all about touring on the road and the situation when electricity is somehow cut off and we leave it to B. J. and his drum solo to keep things going until we get the power back on'.

But the lyric is about more than this. It's the rigours of touring as seen from the viewpoint not of the band or the roadies but of their abused and battered equipment. Brooker's song was chipper enough to get on a single and open side two of the album, but it was merely a vehicle for Wilson. The trouble is there's no authenticity. Unlike the rest of the song, Wilson's solo is in 5/4 time from the start and is subject to overdubs that obfuscate the power the drummer could *really* bring to the situation. It's a mess, but then so is the song, which merely repeats the tape of one verse (as The Beatles had done the previous year on 'I Me Mine') to bulk out the time. The best moment is a burst of audience applause flown in from a live concert at Felt Forum, during which Wilson shouts 'Rubbish!' at his own solo.

'Song For A Dreamer' (Trower, Reid)

The first masterpiece in Trower's career is so fully out of step with the rest of the album that it seems to belong to a different band altogether and to have been inspired by a dream of the deep other than the rotting corpses and weeping oilskins that populate Reid's imagination. And yet, the words *are* Reid's, and on the surface, they sit perfectly in the same graveyard as *Home*. This is a song about death on an operating table. Like a continuation of 'The Dead Man's Dream', Reid carries the patient's spirit from the hospital to chill seas where 'our friend the Arab' (a reference to Captain Ahab in *Moby-Dick* as filtered through the 'Captain Arab' of 'Bob Dylan's 115th Dream') joins him forever in dark and haunted billows. And you're invited there too.

As quoted by *Zigzag* in 1976, Trower remembered that the words and lyric were created independently, but both turned out to be about Jimi Hendrix: 'I was writing a piece of music in one room, and Keith happened to be writing lyrics in another. So he comes in and says, 'I've got these lyrics, and they're sort of Hendrixy, and maybe we should do a sort of tribute to him'. I said, 'Hey, that's funny, I've got this music".

But this isn't how Trower recalled it in other interviews, where he claimed Reid approached him first, and then he went off and explored Hendrix's music, looking for something that would fit. For example, he told *classicrockpage.com* in 2000:

> I felt I had better study his playing 'cause we wanted it to be an obvious tribute. So I borrowed some albums and sat and listened to them. There were two or three tracks that really, really got into my subconscious. One of them was '1983' from *Electric Ladyland*. 'Song For A Dreamer' really comes from that. 'Song For A Dreamer' showed a style I could be creative with as a guitar player, and that was when I started to really get Hendrix's influences very, very strong.

Trower's result is a wallowing but weighty nudge at the ocean floor that functions as a second instalment in Hendrix's submarine epic, only *now* the mermaids are all gone and the sea's littered with the broken backs of wrecked ships and their gnarly, barnacled, undead denizens. The track has a murky potency, tugged by monstrous tides in which ranks of overdubbed guitars yawn like harpooned whales. It's not quite Hendrix, of course (Trower was just the first of a long line of guitarists who were not quite Hendrix), but it's the trippiest Procol Harum ever became: a piece made for psychic contemplation on an album otherwise bereft of mind expansion.

As a sonic adventure, it's incredible. As a springboard, it's impeccable. 'Song For A Dreamer' gave Trower the confidence to step out on his own – a cheap-suit Hendrix for sure, but one who had suddenly, if belatedly, discovered his soul.

'Playmate Of The Mouth' (Brooker, Reid)
The rest of side two is such a let-down that 'Song For A Dreamer' surely should have come last. Then we could have told a better story about how *Broken Barricades* saw Trower stepping out on his own. Lyrically, 'Playmate Of The Mouth' is a second dive into the sexual preoccupations of 'Luskus Delph', but without that track's cunning invention. There's one overt carnal image – 'baby sandwich soaped for comfort' – but it's disagreeable, and the images are all wrong. We seem to be at some deep-South funeral where the guests have curdled memories of transgressions with Savage Rose, likely a whore. The title may be a mix of the *Playboy* centrefold and oral sex, but it's hard to tell Reid's intentions here.

There's little Brooker could do to rescue this one, so he simply played up the New Orleans feel on a detuned upright piano, added an uncredited clutch of trumpet and trombone players, and let Trower run loose on stinging lines over the top.

'Poor Mohammed' (Trower, Reid)
Trower's third feature and second vocal is by-the-book blues with bottleneck slide and overdubbed guitar solos. It's the album's one track you can skip without feeling you've missed anything, so it's awkward indeed that it's the last. The one instrumental surprise is how precisely it predicts side one of Led Zeppelin's *Physical Graffiti* from four years later.

The words are unpleasant, even by *Broken Barricades* standards. For the second time, after having sung about 'our friend the Arab' (pronounced eye-rab) on 'Song For A Dreamer', Trower mentions Moslems, and this time, it's not pretty. Mohammed, in Reid's vitriolic verse, is a male equivalent of 'Simple Sister', to whom much the same maltreatment is meted out. For the crime of being an elderly voyeur (and remembering that we've just attended a 'voyeur's ball' in 'Playmate Of The Mouth'), he's kicked downstairs; his holy books are burned, he's made to lick food from the floor, and, finally, he's imprisoned in the cellar to be eaten by rats.

Procol Harum Live: In Concert With The Edmonton Symphony Orchestra (1972)

Personnel:
Dave Ball: guitar
Gary Brooker: piano, vocals
Alan Cartwright: bass
Chris Copping: organ
B.J. Wilson: drums
The Edmonton Symphony Orchestra: conducted by Lawrence Leonard
Da Camera Singers: vocals
Recorded: 18 November 1971, Northern Alberta Jubilee Auditorium, Edmonton,
Canada
Producer: Chris Thomas
Label: A&M (US), Chrysalis (UK)
Release date: April 1972
Charts: US: 5, UK: 48
Running time: 41:36 (A: 22:38, B: 18:58)

For a band as precarious as Procol Harum, a live album at this point made little artistic sense. Yet *Procol Harum Live* somehow managed a magical thing. (The actual title is something of a mystery, given the variants on the record labels almost everywhere.) It rejuvenated the band, going on to sell an astonishing 500,000 copies, and even spawned a hit single. As a consequence, even the old material began charting again. Today, we look back on the album as the last landmark of a group that continued to tour, make records, and even have a minor success or two, but they never much troubled the public consciousness again.

Understanding the album's appeal leads us into a complex dance with its year, which saw the beginning of another landmark: that of the slow rise and somewhat swifter fall of prog rock. Though 1973/1974 saw prog's brief chart dominance thanks to million-sellers like *The Dark Side Of The Moon* and *Tubular Bells*, it was 1972 when the symphonic style of adult rock was at its height. This was the year of Emerson, Lake & Palmer's *Trilogy*, Family's *Bandstand*, Genesis's *Foxtrot*, Gentle Giant's *Octopus*, Jethro Tull's *Thick As A Brick*, Strawbs' *Grave New World*, Uriah Heep's *Demons And Wizards*, Wishbone Ash's *Argus* and Yes's *Close To The Edge*. Good company all, and you'd certainly have *Procol Harum Live* in your collection if you had those albums. But it couldn't have been just prog rock fans who were buying 'Conquistador'. This was also the year that glam came of age: the peak of an infatuation with glittered-up rock 'n' roll on both sides of the Atlantic. There was an odd nostalgia at play, as long as it was nostalgia reinvented as sonic confectionary. Audiences wanted a future that was rooted comfortably in the past. They wanted stars that strutted in boas while singing old-style songs.

Procol Harum Live also fed into this, though notably, it didn't have *that song* in its grooves.

The band had changed again since *Broken Barricades*. Big Bertha guitarist Dave Ball had replaced Trower and finding themselves too restricted as the four-piece, they'd added new bassist Alan Cartwright, enabling Copping to concentrate on organ. Returned to their classic format, they were finally able to repeat the orchestral crossover they'd presented at Stratford, Canada, in 1969. In fact, the only reason the *Procol Harum Live* album happened at all was that this wasn't just another knock-off memento of a live gig. It was a big deal: a high-profile, expensive event involving a full orchestra and choir. The live album was intended to claw back some of the expenses. Reid told *Sounds* in 1973: 'It was a terrible risk. If it hadn't been a success at all, we'd have lost over $60,000. The group would have been in so much debt we'd have had to split up. It would have meant the end of Procol Harum. We gambled that it would be about as successful as *Broken Barricades* in selling power, and that would be okay'.

Nevertheless, the event was rushed and ill-prepared since it happened halfway through an American tour. This time, Brooker didn't have the luxury of sitting at his grand piano for weeks and writing out arrangements. So he dusted off the orchestrations he'd created for Stratford and distributed them to the new players. But that wasn't enough for a full concert. He told to *SongwriterUniverse* in 2020:

On the plane flying up to Edmonton, I thought, 'We don't have songs that are up-tempo'. By then we had 'In Held 'Twas In I', 'A Salty Dog' and 'Whaling Stories'. They were dramatic and descriptive, but they weren't up-tempo and in your face. And so, I thought, 'How about 'Conquistador'?'. It was up-tempo, and there was something that came into my head of dramatising it and giving a bit of life to it. So, I adapted the tune as it stood and wrote an introduction to set the scene. That's what that orchestral introduction is, with the trumpet over it. And 'Conquistador' was always a short song: three short verses and repeat choruses. That's why, in the middle of it, we went back and redid half of the intro, and it gives it a break. Then the orchestra comes back in and it all settles down to the last verse.

Reid told *Zigzag* in 1973:

(Brooker) was still writing the orchestrations on the plane to Edmonton. He didn't write the orchestration for 'Conquistador' until a couple of days before we did the concert. He'd certainly not heard them played until the day of the concert – in fact, the actual concert itself. What we wanted to do was get there a couple of days in advance and rehearse and also get the technical problems sorted out for recordings, but it eventually ended up that we couldn't really rehearse. In fact, one song on the album we had never played before with an orchestra until we actually did it. That was 'All This and More' and 'Conquistador' I don't think we actually rehearsed with the orchestra. They had played the orchestration and rehearsed it once, but I don't think we actually went through it with them. So, we didn't have a satisfactory rehearsal in any way before we actually went on stage.

Brooker recalled the concert as a piling-up of blunders. He told *Rolling Stone* in 1972:

That afternoon, there was to be a full rehearsal: choir, orchestra and us. When we got there, we found out that the choir was an amateur one. They had daytime jobs, so they weren't going to be at the rehearsal. Then, our equipment was stopped in customs and didn't arrive for this full rehearsal, so it ended up with just the piano and the organ rehearsing with the orchestra, running it through. So, that wasn't really a rehearsal. The following day, our equipment was there and we had a full rehearsal for three hours. Only about 45 minutes of that was the whole thing because the choir had to come in on their lunch break.

As feared, the concert was a mess. The rehearsals the band *did* have saw Brooker clash with the conductor and Ball's amp played up. The Musician's Union leaned on everybody. The band were nervous and made mistakes (Brooker's spoonerism 'and though the cloud crapped furiously' is rightly infamous), and band and orchestra were so poorly integrated that Wilson had to have wing mirrors mounted on his kit to see the conductor. But by and large, the orchestra and choir rose to the occasion – not at all a given when dinner suits clash with rock groups – and somehow Wally Heider and Chris Thomas got it all down beautifully on tape.

The full set was this: Copping solo playing 'The Adagio D'Albinoni' with the orchestra (see the chapter of that title later in this book), then the band came in for 'Conquistador', 'Whaling Stories', 'Luskus Delph', 'Shine On Brightly', 'All This And More' and 'In Held 'Twas In I'. The encore was 'Repent Walpurgis'. Thomas then requested that they repeat some of the material to ensure they could release error-free recordings, so Brooker gave the audience the option of hanging around to hear duplicate performances of 'Conquistador', 'Whaling Stories' (twice: the first try incomplete) and the entire 'In Held 'Twas In I'. The final album was assembled with numerous splices between the versions.

It could have flopped, hubris to yet more Neanderthal pretensions. But miraculously, the album received positive reviews – the exact opposite of the savagery that greeted the band last time they dared work with an orchestra. *Rolling Stone* was uncharacteristically effusive:

Someone might easily turn up his nose at this approach and dismiss it as precious, transparent, even comical. But an understanding of and a sympathy with Procol Harum's attitude leads one to accept this album as the group's most forthright admission so far that their music is indeed excessively grandiose, unsubtle, and often marked by a fine sense of comedy (usually self-directed). It also happens to be among the most viscerally powerful and emotionally devastating music available.

Chrysalis in the UK and A&M in the US promoted the album with a vengeance. 'Conquistador' gained radio traction and rose to 22 in the UK and 16 in the US, even though anybody who wanted the song could find it and much more of the same style on the album. And though all the material was old, it was as if listeners were hearing the band *correctly* for the first time. Unsurprisingly, Procol Harum henceforth became one of that select body of artists whose careers were punctuated by orchestral events, even if they (bafflingly) failed to capitalise on their new fame with an orchestral tour. Also, unsurprisingly, it wasn't the stripped-down R&B of *Broken Barricades* that the band chose to move forward with but elaborate symphonic rock – at least for a while.

The live album might be their best seller, but it hasn't seen much in the way of expanded reissues. We haven't had a single extra second of music from the concert. We *do* have some of the rehearsals, and they're all wretched, except for 'A Salty Dog', which is an improvement on the concert: the orchestra and choir are mixed more sensitively. The rehearsal version of 'Luskus Delph' has a somewhat muted flavour, as if the extra players had only just realised what the song was about.

'Conquistador' (Brooker, Reid)

It's always surprising what does and doesn't catch on. Many pop successes seem to be accidental due to luck or simple sustained promotion. This hit live version of a song then five years old gained its commercial power not from the lyric or melody (which were good enough the *first* time around, you'd suppose) but from Brooker's exuberant orchestral arrangement, which adds dramatic galloping strings and bright slabs of Mariachi brass. The result is a comical overload, culminating in dentist-drill sirens. The one sour note is Ball's scribbly solo, added in post-production and apparently inferior to what he played on the night.

'Whaling Stories' (Brooker, Reid)

This epic was made for grand treatment – if it had been on *A Salty Dog*, it surely would have gotten it – and though this reading lacks the clarity of the studio version, it packs a far greater sonic punch thanks to its sumptuous cinematic integration of strings in the opening section, the bellowing brass intrusions as the storm mounts, and an infernal sequence that sees Brooker somehow marshalling all the voices at his disposal without them overwhelming the piece. Ball is again the track's weakest contributor. This section would have worked just as well without his screeching over the top. But woodwind birdsong gracefully evokes dawn, and the anthem – with full-on orchestra and choir – is truly uplifting.

'A Salty Dog' (Brooker, Reid)

The LP cover makes a big deal of the quadraphonic seagull sound effects used here (an idea the band stole from Pink Floyd), but the album was not originally released in quad, and to date, no multi-channel version has been made available. Already having laid down a perfect orchestral 'A Salty Dog' in the studio, there was little chance of this bettering it, but there was also no chance of it not being performed. It's all a little overbearing, neutering the bittersweet sorrow of the original. If only Brooker had dared to perform it without the band – just his voice and the orchestra and choir.

'All This And More' (Brooker, Reid)

Though this piece was included simply because Brooker already had an orchestral arrangement written, there is nevertheless a point to the track since Fisher had omitted that arrangement from *A Salty Dog*. Here's what it *could* have sounded like. There's almost no sign of the extra performers through the bulk of the song, but they pile in vigorously during the 'Come Lollard, raise your lute and sing' verse, with massed brass accents and a wordless keening choir.

'In Held 'Twas In I' (Brooker, Fisher, Reid)

It's what we're all here for: a side-filling rendition of the band's most expansive work with a sumptuous prog-rock arrangement. Up to this point, an entire rendition wasn't part of the band's live repertoire. From here on, it would be a fixture at orchestral concerts. *Procol Harum Live* finally sets the piece among the pantheon of prog's greats, even if you will most certainly never pick up a copy of *Prog* or *Classic Rock* magazines and see it listed in the 'best of' countdowns. It works terrifically well, all the way from the opening choir and string drones to the final hall-shattering orchestral stab. In particular, ''Twas Teatime at the Circus' is a riot and seems to settle everyone into the piece's craziness: there's a notable uptick in engagement thereafter. The rest of the suite ricochets from mood to mood with an intensity almost unique among the track's peers.

'Luskus Delph' (Brooker, Reid)

This was released only on the B-side of the 'Conquistador' single in the UK and select other territories (the US and elsewhere got 'A Salty Dog' instead). Again, an orchestral arrangement already existed, so it was easily adapted for the concert. Fittingly, the horns take the lead, even if what they add sounds uncomfortably like a group of huntsmen homing in on a fox.

Grand Hotel (1973)

Personnel:
Gary Brooker: piano, banjo, vocals
Alan Cartwright: bass, acoustic guitar, percussion
Chris Copping: organ, banjo
Mick Grabham: electric guitar
B.J. Wilson: drums, mandolin
Christiane Legrand: vocals ('Fires (Which Burnt Brightly)')
Recorded: April–November 1972, AIR Studios, London
Producer: Chris Thomas
Label: Chrysalis
Release date: March 1973
Charts: US: 21
Running time: 41:14 (A: 19:01, B: 22:13)

Whoever Brooker thought was buying *Procol Harum Live*, its critical acclaim, even in parts of the more fusty press, must have suggested a means forward out of the grub of the rock 'n' roll crowd and into the more gentrified realms of establishment music. If so, he was hardly alone since bands like Pink Floyd and King Crimson were busy making the same calculation in 1973. When Procol Harum reformed in 1991, they occupied an enviable space, capable of presenting themselves as a fine vintage of a band that even the highbrow could appreciate. They played arty venues, classical music festivals, fetes, and country outings where there was more the clink of champagne glasses than applause. Brooker might have even believed this possible in the 1970s, but he was mistaken. The whole concept of classical rock was soon in for a rude awakening. In the meantime, there was an awkward balance to be achieved between the college bedrock (educated for sure but demanding a *little* rowdy excitement) and the intelligentsia.

Grand Hotel aimed straight down that middle. It saw a band energised by belated success – Brooker out of the doldrums of *Broken Barricades* and capable of writing the entire album's music by himself, Reid, whose lyrics were less queasy and more poetically restrained, and players that verged on virtuoso. Brooker told *Prog* in 2018: 'Most of the *Grand Hotel* songs are quite split-personality things that change mood. There are almost two songs in every song. We thought we'd have that big, lush sound. It wasn't all done with orchestra, but there was quite a bit. We did use some outside influences, like Christiane Legrand on 'Fires (Which Burn Brightly)'. She was a French jazz improviser but was also from The Swingle Singers, who had done a lot of classical interpretations'.

He told *New Musical Express* in 1973: 'So far, from people's remarks, it seems to be the first one we've done which hasn't one or two songs which don't quite come together for some reason or another, or some recording faults and so on. And that's what any group's working for, trying to make the best album that's ever been'.

With its country home cover shots and lavish lyric book, the album radiated European high class. It wasn't the first time a Procol Harum album had a cover based on the title track (the same was true of the UK *Shine On Brightly* and *A Salty Dog*), but the imagery made it look like something right on the zeitgeist of 1973: a concept album. It wasn't any more than those others had been, but for once, Reid was willing to contemplate the conceit. He told *Sounds* in 1973: 'It's not a concept album as such, although the cover work may be deceptive as far as that goes. Originally, I thought the title of that track would be great for the album title, and started writing the song – well, it's not as blasé as that sounds! I'd really like to do a concept, but I feel if I did, I'd have to be very deliberate and write it as one would a book'.

He elaborated for *Zigzag* the same year: 'It isn't a concept album. It was just that, for the first time, we echoed the particular song in the artwork and everything, and I guess in the promotion of the album in relationship to the song. I'd like for us to do, not an opera as such, but something like that. A concept kind of album, yes. I think it's the sort of thing we could do well'.

As usual, *Grand Hotel* was born of strife. Sessions began before *Procol Harum Live* was released. It was Dave Ball's first time in the studio with the band (and his first major session at all), and for reasons that are still unclear, he didn't work out. Brooker told the press that Ball's playing wasn't up to muster, but the truth appears to be that he had a physical altercation with Wilson. Yet again, the entire initial album sessions were scrapped (though again, there are conflicting opinions over whether any of the Ball sessions were used on the final album). Desperate calls brought in Mick Grabham of Cochise – humorously, too late for the cover shot, so his head had to be pasted onto Ball's body. There was a much brighter atmosphere all around now that the financial gamble of the live album was paying off (and a surprise hit single surely helped), and at last, there was a stability that would endure more or less until the band's dissolution in 1977. Grabham might look like he had the demeanour of Matthew Fisher, but he played like a dream, and even smiled on occasion.

Chrysalis pushed *Grand Hotel* hard on both sides of the Atlantic. There were two singles, lavish junkets and giveaways. There were also more high-profile orchestral concerts, this time at London's Rainbow Theatre with the Royal Philharmonic and the Hollywood Bowl with the Los Angeles Philharmonic. There was heavy press coverage and billboards. Those stiffs in morning suits were everywhere. And the album did...zip. It sold well, but it didn't cause even a ripple of interest over the sullen black pond of the British public consciousness. Things were better in the US, where it actually charted despite *Rolling Stone* making it abundantly clear which side of the highbrow/lowbrow argument they stood on: '*Grand Hotel* is a collection of overblown production jobs that, at their worst, approach self-parody, and simpler, less grandiose tracks that suggest Procol Harum may yet find a way out of the corner they have worked themselves into'.

But you could feel the band's expectations deflating. *Procol Harum Live* had been a blip, not a new platform. Let the struggle commence yet again.

'Grand Hotel' (Brooker, Reid)
Procol Harum's last charting US single of the 1970s should have done much better, given that it was simply 'Conquistador' painted in even broader strokes. It's as gorgeously orchestrated as the highlights of *Procol Harum Live*. Was it just *too much*, even for FM radio? Brooker explained to *SongwriterUniverse* in 2020: 'The Edmonton album was very successful, and not just for the money, but artistically. In particular, the song 'Grand Hotel' was crying out for an orchestra. It was pretty epic. So we recorded that song with an orchestra, and we did that with a choir as well'.

His now-standard method of building anthems was to start small with a solo piano riff and build and build until the record groove strained with the sound. Here, a plaintive melody lulls you into thinking this is a lament for a lost lover, only to disarm you with triumphant chords and abrupt detours into waltz time as if we're back in 'A Whiter Shade Of Pale' snatched into seasick cartwheels across a glittering ballroom floor to the accompaniment of a vast, imperious choir multitracked until it seems like the whole room is choked with singing. As if all that isn't disorientating enough, at 2:58, Brooker throws in a contrasting sequence for weeping choir and mandolins played by Wilson, building to an overpowering melodramatic crescendo, only to shift gears again at 4:05 into a monstrous dance of the damned. It all culminates in an overload of classical rock that, had it had the slightest hint of a snigger in Brooker's voice, would be the most ridiculous thing you've ever heard. And yet, somehow, it works, and it works magnificently.

Lost in all this rococo is a lyric celebrating the lavish lifestyles of the rich patrons of a frosty pile in the country. Reid's words are sneaky, listing the *accoutrements* of ostentatious wealth ('Dover sole and oeufs Mornay, profiteroles and peach flambé') before insinuating with one more 'Luskus Delph' innuendo that 'French girls' are also on the menu: 'We'll continental slip-and-slide' – and, again, all without the merest whiff of parody. The latter reference grounds the tale at least partially in reality. Procol Harum *did* find themselves in grand hotels while touring Eastern Europe, and there would have been girls on hand. Reid played down these aspects to *Zigzag* in 1973: 'That song is a bit of a fantasy. I'm all for staying in grand hotels and sleeping in silken sheets. None of this out-in-the-country for me, I'm afraid, it's The Ritz'.

Brooker was more forthright to *Songfacts* in 2010:

It's actually an autobiographical Procol Harum on-the-road song. But the grandeur of the words, and then all the expressions used of the food and wine and sparkle and chandelier, I looked at that and thought, well, you've got to conjure up an atmosphere here. And having experienced the same things that Keith had experienced in what he was writing about, I was able to interpret – hopefully – his lyrics into something which enhanced the whole effect.

A version of the track stripped of orchestra and choir was released on the album's *40 Years* edition in 2009 and is revelatory: you won't miss them at all. What's exposed is an assured band performance that was sumptuous enough all by itself.

'Toujours L'Amour' (Brooker, Reid)

From one set of French girls to another. Reid's sour lyric documents the aftermath of a relationship and the singer's decision either to rent a villa in France and enjoy the local talent or go off to Spain and shoot himself in the head. Maybe it was down to a coin toss. Referring to the line, 'She'd left me a note and taken the cat', Reid assured *Zigzag* in 1973 that it wasn't autobiographical: 'I've still got the cat'. But that could be typical Reid wordplay. Procol Harum was named after a cat. Is it possible that this is a song about troubles in the band?

Musically, it's all *Home*-style muscle, overlain with a closely double-tracked Brooker vocal, suggesting it might have been considered as a possible single in the Jethro Tull vein. Grabham gets his first solos on a Procol Harum song, again giddy with overdub, and his fat sound works brilliantly.

'A Rum Tale' (Brooker, Reid)

There's a third option open to the protagonist of 'Toujours L'Amour', and that's to drown his sorrows. Here's another song of escape from the unmentionable 'she' who caused all this woe: absconding to a tropical island and oblivion in a liquor glass shaped like a coconut. Brooker arranges it as an upbeat piano ballad in a sing-along 6/8 but neglects to put much interest into the melody or thought into an arrangement that trades almost entirely on Procol Harum of the 1967 vintage.

'T.V. Ceasar' (Brooker, Reid)

Reid's misspelling is consistent and, hence, likely purposeful but has never been explained. There may *possibly* be some pun on the words 'cease' or 'ceasefire', but the song itself makes it clear that the word meant is 'Caesar'. It's a depiction of television as the tinpot dictator that lords it over us all. Reid told *Zigzag* about the song in 1973: 'That comes from being in America a lot. They have these talk shows. Particularly a couple of years ago when David Frost was really popular there and Johnny Carson and Joey Bishop and all those shows, and the idea of the song was like they are all TV Caesars: Caesars of the television. They're running everything. We've never talked on one of those shows, but that's our ambition'.

The last sentence somewhat negates the criticism, but Reid's assertion that TV controls the public and, hence, political discourse in America is correct even if today it's not talk shows that bend opinions but news anchors. Just as you'd need to know British TV in the 1970s to understand Pink Floyd's 'And I mean that most sincerely' in 'Have A Cigar', you'd also need to recognise David Frost's mannerisms here. The trouble is, it's not a very good lyric by Reid's standards – a presaging of the more direct way of writing that he would increasingly adopt from this point onwards. And once you've grasped the thrust of his diatribe, the words have nothing new to offer over the rest of the 5:50 the track runs.

The songwriting mannerism is repeated yet again here: start on solo piano, then shove in the band. Brooker's tune is pretty in the verses but less so in the chorus. The huge orchestral production (meant to end side one with the same wallop with which it began) is misplaced, and the song holds together less well than 'Grand Hotel'. Grabham gives the song excitement with another chunky solo, but it's too short and too early, and afterwards, the song has nowhere to go except back over the same old ground.

'A Souvenir Of London' (Brooker, Reid)
Three earlier Procol Harum albums began their second sides with a track that was in contrast to all the others. Here's a fun return of the habit: a jug-band stomp with banjos and spoons that was meant to sound like a cross between hitmakers Mungo Jerry and a one-man band. Reid's lyric makes it clear that the souvenir in question is a dose of the clap, though a comment to UCLA Radio in 2002 was revealing on the way his thought processes worked: 'One time, I can remember I was wanting to write a song, and I'm just holding a pencil, and the pencil says 'A souvenir of London' on it. So that inspired me to write a song'.

The song angled for a novelty single in the UK, but airplay was out of the question, and the lowbrow wit put a dent in the album's class. Still, official live recordings and footage show that the band translated the song well into performance: all huddled at the front of the stage with their unaccustomed instruments and having the time of their lives.

'Bringing Home The Bacon' (Brooker, Reid)
The odious lyrics Reid had been writing intermittently since *Broken Barricades* reach a low point here. The song is simply a collection of food fragments that, on the surface, seem to be about an overfed child. But Reid said it was actually a commentary on the gluttony he witnessed in the US: the 'milk-fed baby dumpling' is an obese adult, waddling around an American supermarket loading up the cart or squeezing behind a bolted-down restaurant table. The album's second track of vitriol about US culture, it's presumably meant to contrast that country against the refined (and positively rendered) consumption of diners at the grand European hotel of the title track, though, in truth, they're aspects of the same disease.

There's a lot more fun to be had in the arrangement, which slops around Wilson's cowbell and Brooker's full-bellied bass riff and erupts into sudden wide-throated, maddeningly catchy recorder shrills, credited mischievously to The Pahene Recorder Ensemble. They're actually just the band. The Ensemble is named after Harry Pahene, Brooker's father's stage name.

'For Liquorice John' (Brooker, Reid)

Brooker's school friend Dave Mundy has a small part in the Procol Harum story. As a kid, he thought up the band name Liquorice John Death and the title and cover for an album to be called *Ain't Nothin' To Get Excited About*. In 1997, when Procol Harum released an album of R&B covers recorded during the *Home* sessions (see the 'Beyond These Things' chapter at the end of this book), they used all three of Mundy's ideas. But his mental health issues had overwhelmed him in 1970, and he jumped to his death off a building in Southend. Reid never knew him, but nevertheless wrote 'For Liquorice John' as mythology, much as he'd mythologised Jimi Hendrix's death in 'Song For A Dreamer'. The doctor is back, and so is the transportation of the soul from ground to sea. But there's no redemption in the deep this time, merely a conscious echo of Stevie Smith's poem 'Not Waving But Drowning', which Reid claimed was autobiographical. Reid had also found himself in trouble in the water and been mistaken for larking about. Smith died in 1971, so it's likely the song forms a eulogy on multiple levels. Reid certainly tried to write the words with Smith's simplicity and clarity rather than his own more nuanced allusiveness.

But as *sound*, this is a world away from Trower's gentle wake for a lost soul. Brooker's piano is jangly and strident, his tune is perfunctory, and the chords smear into astringency – the final crash chord bringing back chilling memories of 'The Dead Man's Dream' – and the one place where an orchestra might have been appropriate is bereft of it.

'Fires (Which Burnt Brightly)' (Brooker, Reid)

Here's the castle of 'Broken Barricades' in the process of being burst asunder – a metaphor for the kind of domestic argument that might lead to the breakup documented in 'Toujours L'Amour'. Reid tells us there's nothing left of love except the routine of inflicting harm on each other. In the programme to the Hollywood Bowl concert, he was asked about the nature of the conflict. He replied: 'It's a relationship, like between a husband and wife bickering and thinking of divorce. They're still fighting, but the war is already lost. The causes are well in the past, and they're fighting ghosts'.

Long before, such thoughts would have led him to a brutal self-examination of the kind he wrote in 'Homburg'. Here's an older and more weary Keith Reid, resigned to the struggle and lacking even the energy to sunder it for good. It's an excellent piece of writing, and in its final line, 'Our poems and letters have turned to deceptions', is as wrenching a commentary on failed romance as you're likely to hear. The one fire still left to burn is the one that consumes all that paper.

The most startling thing about Brooker's arrangement is the inclusion of Christiane Legrand of The Swingle Singers: an actual French girl who overdubbed layers of improvised vocals on top, essentially repeating that ensemble's old act of vocalising Bach lines as light jazz in exactly the same way that Jacques Loussier did on piano. The Singers had even teamed up with The Modern Jazz Quartet in 1966 on a delightful version of 'Air On A G String' that sounds like a flock of Parisian pigeons all bobbing their heads together. Brooker gives Legrand a jumpy Bach melody to dance around, lifting an otherwise mundane song immeasurably. There's a knotty set of central variations for prog fans to dissect, but the greatest joy is Legrand's scat singing towards the end, which those same fans will detest.

'Robert's Box' (Brooker, Reid)

The innuendo in The Beatles' 'Doctor Robert' is that he's actually prescribing recreational drugs. It's the first of three drug songs on side two of *Revolver*. Reid knew the song – *everybody* knew the song – and so there's no chance that *his* Robert (also a drug-dispensing doctor) wasn't a nod back to it. But 'doctor' here is also used as slang for dealer, and the singer is an addict with a foot in the door, desperate for a little unprescribed something from the doctor's 'magic box'.

Imagine Brooker receiving the lyric from Reid in 1972 and wondering what to match to it. Something scarifying and desperate? Something mean and brooding? Velvet Underground drones or *Psycho* violins? His solution was a Latin rhythm with Hawaiian guitars, grass-skirted singers, and a comedy baritone vocal in the chorus. No, I can't imagine Procol Harum performing any of this in a wintry London studio, either. At 2:54, the piece diverts into a contrasting section for massed guitars, evoking a different Beatles era: the triumphal need for a different kind of fix on *Abbey Road*.

Exotic Birds And Fruit (1974)

Personnel:
Gary Brooker: piano, acoustic guitar, marimba, vocals
Mick Grabham: electric and acoustic guitar
Chris Copping: organ, banjo
Alan Cartwright: bass
B.J. Wilson: drums, mandolin
B.J. Cole: pedal steel ('As Strong As Sampson')
Recorded: 1973-1974, AIR Studios, London, UK
Producer: Chris Thomas
Label: Chrysalis
Release date: April 1974
Charts: US: 86
Running time: 37:04 (A: 18:05, B: 18:59)

Though the handsome cover by 17th-century still-life painter Jakob Bogdani
and the title that was named after it both suggest an album even more regal
than the finer tracks on *Grand Hotel*, the album itself is a continuation of
the worst. Reid's lyrics are a one-note catalogue of disillusion. And having
attempted to ride the symphonic prog wave on *Grand Hotel*, Brooker now
purposefully stripped the band back to basics. He told *Goldmine* in 2010: 'We
always liked to do something different. I remember after *Grand Hotel*, we all
thought, 'We've done the orchestral bit, we've done it live at Edmonton, we've
done the studio version of that with the orchestrations on the *Grand Hotel*
album. That was a bright, big production. Let's go back to being a rock 'n' roll
band'. That's where *Exotic Birds And Fruit* was at. We went back to being a
five-piece band that just recorded live in the studio'.

Reid told *Circus* in 1974: 'We found ourselves categorised in most people's
minds as a classical rock band, and we were expected to live up to it. We
really aren't that much of a classically oriented band. It's always nice to use
an occasional orchestration if it fits in, but it becomes very tiresome having
to answer for it for the rest of your life. On this new album, we are trying to
dispel that symphonic image'.

It was a perverse reaction, given that the 'symphonic image' had already
proved it could reap dividends.

Despite the shifting approaches, one thing never changed: strife in the
studio. Though the lineup was stable, the band were back at their familiar
home at AIR – and 24-track tape enabled them to be meticulous and
spontaneous – producer Chris Thomas didn't have his mind on the work.
He'd been distracted by the much greater pleasures of mixing Pink Floyd's
The Dark Side Of The Moon over at Abbey Road and didn't find Procol
Harum's songs inspiring or have much to offer to enliven them. The result
tended to be more of what had afflicted parts of *Grand Hotel*: slight songs
thickened by bombast. It was Thomas's last work for the band.

The sessions threw yet another curveball their way. This time, it was the oil crisis, a near-paralytic strike, three-day weeks, sudden power cuts, and shortages that – ironically – ended up as one of the first nails in the coffin for prog rock. The immediate effect was deleterious – a curtailing of the lavish packaging (making LPs far less of an art object for fans) and a thinning and cheapening of the vinyl itself, which wrecked the market for hi-fi devotees. The industry knee-jerked by deciding that singles were the way forward and leaned on its artists to commercialise.

Procol Harum didn't know it at the time, but the less-ornate sound of *Exotic Birds And Fruit* was the future. It was just a shame it didn't work for them. Maybe a less grandiose cover would have helped sell the band. It certainly could have prevented *Rolling Stone* from bludgeoning an album it hardly seemed bothered to play: '*Exotic Birds And Fruit* is another slab of false majesty for which this band has become noted – elephantine, grandiose production, pretentious, empty lyrics, and the sort of artistic posturing that would embarrass Ted Baxter. Procol Harum is a perfect example of a band that has outlived its usefulness'.

This couldn't have helped morale, which was bottoming out yet again, giving Reid even more reason for downbeat lyrics and Wilson more reason to drown his problems in drink. The lead single 'Nothing But The Truth' tanked, the album fared worse than the last one, and the band's fortunes took a downturn once more, this time decisively. This is the point where many less-committed fans bail. It's a case of diminishing returns, patchy work, and little of the old fire or invention. It's workmanlike for sure, with a particularly strong first side but precious few masterpieces. The industry agreed, not bothering to release this or its successors on CD for years during the CD boom and only eventually providing extended sets for the most fanatical of completists.

'Nothing But The Truth' (Brooker, Reid)
This anthemic pomp with a buffed-up, bright production that cries out for airplay was intended as the album's calling card. It does everything right – fast, big chorus, modern sound, even touches of inoffensive strings – but it still feels superficial. It *could* have been a fluke hit, but it didn't really deserve to be. Of course, it flopped, and you can't blame the band's name or Reid's resolutely downbeat lyric for turning listeners off. The song is simply exhausting to hear.

'Beyond The Pale' (Brooker, Reid)
Another single, another miss. Here, Brooker digs into his continental mannerisms, as quoted by *DISCoveries* in 1992: 'It's kind of Eastern European. It does pop up now and again. I guess one of the Liszt pieces is always banging around in my head'.

The slow polka rhythm gives the song a confident swagger that – like 'Nothing But The Truth' – awkwardly contrasts with Reid's sour lyric, which is a fruitless struggle through life's miseries in the hope of spiritual gold. The title doesn't appear in the song (Brooker sings 'beyond the veil' in the second line), but it's impossible to think of a man as introverted as Reid not referring back to a single that still hung albatross-like around the band's necks.

'As Strong As Samson' (Brooker, Reid)

Strike out: three in a row. For all that, 'As Strong As Samson' is significantly better than its two predecessors, thanks to a less-hungry production that merely updates the classic Procol Harum sound to the fatter mid-1970s norm – particularly Wilson's chunky kit, which he thrashes delightedly just to see what it sounds like. There's a memorable tune and neat pedal steel touches by an underutilised B. J. Cole from Grabham's old band Cochise.

Reid has a little more to say, too, in verses that fling creative invective at everyone from psychiatrists, lawyers, bankers, stockbrokers, preachers, and TV stations to 'Black men and white men/And Arabs and Jews' squabbling for dominance. The only problem here is the title, which is obscure even in context. I *think* Reid is implying that we can overcome all the negative influences on our lives if we're determined enough to pull the whole unholy edifice down, but it doesn't make a lot of sense. Samson perished, too, and so most likely would we. For radio listeners who merely needed someone to tell them how to think, the allusion by itself was fatal. The single (issued in 1976 long after the album had been and gone) tried to clarify matters by adding a parenthetical title: 'As Strong As Samson (When You're Being Held To Ransom)'. But that just makes it worse.

'The Idol' (Brooker, Reid)

The album's epic is modest in length (6:37) but grandiose in production, starting as usual with solo piano and building overdub by overdub into a veritable cathedral of sound for a dramatic tail section that fills its entire last three minutes. Brooker lifts his voice to its upper register like he used to, and there are lashings of old-style Hammond and some pleasing Grabham interjections, though he never actually gets a solo.

Reid attempted to decode the lyric for *Circus* in 1974: "'The Idol' is a very mysterious song. It could be about a lot of people, one of them myself. It concerns anybody who desires something enough to worship it, and then through too much adoration of something or somebody, you begin to see that it is really not as magical as you first thought – only a reflection of the hope we carry around inside ourselves and are so eager to squander on any object that catches our fancy'.

So, the song *itself* is the idol, the band is the idol and its writers are the idol. On paper, the narrative is straightforward – a community is threatened, and its inhabitants call on their hero to save them. But he refuses, abandoning them to their fate. We learn no more than this. An illusion is shattered, and that long tail section appears to be the community emerging glassy-eyed into the realisation of the fact. Given that the song follows 'As Strong As Samson', my suspicion is that Reid might have had Richard Nixon in mind, but there were plenty of contenders in 1973.

'The Thin End Of The Wedge' (Brooker, Reid)

The habit of the untypical side-two opener continues here. This is the strangest thing Procol Harum had recorded to that point: an infernal gumbo of creepy-crawly piano chords, King Crimson guitar slurs and muttering background vocals. Reid admitted to *Street Life* in 1976: "The Thin End Of The Wedge' was an experiment lyrically and musically. It doesn't sound much like anything else I've heard. I thought this was something new. However, I was obviously misled in my enthusiasm'.

Not really. It *is* a compelling piece once you submit to its menacing undertow. It would have slotted well into an early Roxy Music album or, for that matter, formed a terrifying adjunct to the domestic arguments on Robert Fripp's *Exposure*. The trouble is that it challenged fan perceptions of the band, nudging them a little too far out of their comfort zone. What is it that distinguishes Procol Harum? Well, it's not this, that's for sure. The truth is that the outside world *and* the fans had long since put the band in a box, and this attempt to be different was equally rejected by both.

'Monsieur R. Monde' (Brooker, Reid)

Alarm bells ring whenever an act riffles through its back catalogue for things to exhume. This composition came from sessions after *A Whiter Shade Of Pale* that were to begin shaping a second album. The 1967 version has been released, along with a number of outtakes from the period, such as 'Seem To Have The Blues (Most Of The Time)', 'Understandably Blue', 'Pandora's Box' (which was also soon to be dusted down for reuse), 'A Robe Of Silk' (eventually re-recorded for *The Well's On Fire*) and 'McGreggor'. Logged under the title 'Monsieur Armand', the original version is up-tempo but undistinguished blues rock, of note mainly for Trower's excellent solo.

There may have been a calculation to burst out of the dank of 'The Thin End Of The Wedge' into this bright pop daylight, and it certainly does dispel the dark mood. But, disappointingly, it also reassures old fans that the band they used to love is still in business since even if the fans didn't know this song prior to *Exotic Birds And Fruit*, they would certainly recognize its mood, big chord changes, and free-form lyric style as vintage Procol Harum.

Reid's words (unchanged from 1967) concern a man who finds himself haunted by the ghost of the title. In the perplexing denouement, we learn that it's actually a manifestation of his own divided psyche and is the good Jekyll part, while he himself is the bad Hyde part. I wonder, could Reid claim not to have read Robert Louis Stevenson?

'Fresh Fruit' (Brooker, Reid)

With the exception of *Home*, every Procol Harum studio album to this point had a title track, and in the original run of albums up to 1977, only *Procol's Ninth* would buck the trend. But what Reid intended by this tribute to fruit is baffling, particularly since the cover painting had apparently come first. I guess if Brian Wilson could write about vegetables, Reid could also give it a shot.

We can remind ourselves of the fruit references Reid had already given us – 'Don't peel no grape/Dream about banana slice' in 'Mabel', 'The peaches snuggle closer down into the clotted cream' in 'Salad Days', 'peach preserve' in 'Luskus Delph', 'bursting grapes' in 'Grand Hotel', and so on – and conclude that there was sex involved. *Disc* mistakenly referred to the album as *Erotic Birds And Fruit* in its review of *Procol's Ninth* in 1975. Look at it one way, and the 'French girls' of 'Grand Hotel' had indeed turned into 'exotic birds' (or even 'erotic birds') with fruity accoutrements ('Fresh fruit, ripe and firm/Makes them squealing taste buds squirm'), and you could even form a creditable treatise that 'makes you want to give up meat' is a nod to lesbianism. But look at it another way, and this is just the praise of healthy living that it *seems* to be.

It's certainly played for laughs, with more of those tropical marimbas from 'Boredom' and barrow-boy whistling to make it clear that the song is another novelty number with one eye on how it would work in promotional videos and as a diversion onstage.

'Butterfly Boys' (Brooker, Reid)

There's no such ambivalence here: Reid's title and lyric are easily deciphered. The band were on the label Chrysalis (a portmanteau of the names of its owners, Chris Wright and Terry Ellis), which had a butterfly as a logo. Just like Procol Harum had complained to the press about Deram and Regal Zonophone, here they were again, complaining about Chrysalis' failures, even though the label had turned *Procol Harum Live* into a massive success and was continuing to do its best for the band even when they delivered albums like *Exotic Birds And Fruit* which weren't going to set the pop business on fire or even recoup much of their costs. Reid snarls at Wright and Ellis: 'We got the groceries, you got the cake'. All would have been forgiven after a hit single, but it does seem unfair that Reid's complaints are all one-sided. To have a hit, you have to have an attractive song, and pieces as snippy as this didn't actually help.

Any suggestion that the band had come into the album sessions on a new high after *Grand Hotel*, or even with a sense of determination to succeed, should be tempered by 'Butterfly Boys', which was actually the first song they recorded. The earlier album had earned their ire, regardless of full-page press ads, billboards, and one-off jaunts to the US to play orchestral concerts at the Hollywood Bowl. Often, when a band declares they're going back to basics in the studio, that's code for a tightened budget, straits imposed on them by a previous lavish gamble that hadn't paid off.

The final irony is that the song is an energetic rocker with a catchy refrain and might have even scored some serious airplay had the words been less negative.

'New Lamps For Old' (Brooker, Reid)

This modest, unassuming song was tagged on the end of the album like a gift to long-suffering 'Pale' devotees. It was written and recorded quickly as if to wrap things up with minimal effort. Familiar chords, tempo, arrangement, and feel lull the listener into the band's unique form of blissful melancholy for four more minutes, in which time stands still just as it did on that far-off single. Reid's lyric is a closing-of-the-day not only for the album but for the very dream of Procol Harum that the song promotes: 'death of the show'. And don't think too hard about the sarcasm implicit in its title.

'Drunk Again' (Brooker, Reid)

The B-side to 'Nothing But The Truth' could have easily bolstered the album, adding a little more value to a skimpy set. Reid's self-denial of the sobriety of 'Whisky Train' rocks hard on Grabham's bricklayer riff and has an infectious rhythm propelled by handclaps and slamming Elton John-style piano chords. But some stumbling, tricky prog touches catch the listener off-guard when all you really want to do is boogie around the living room.

Procol's Ninth (1975)

Personnel:
Gary Brooker: piano, clavinet, marimba, vocals
Alan Cartwright: bass
Chris Copping: organ
Mick Grabham: guitars
B.J. Wilson: drums
Recorded: March-April 1975, Ramport Studio, London, UK
Producers: Jerry Leiber, Mike Stoller
Label: Chrysalis
Release date: August 1975
Charts: US: 52, UK: 41
Running time: 39:19 (A: 19:30, B: 19:49)

If the inference with *Exotic Birds And Fruit* was that Chris Thomas's production left something to be desired because he was losing interest in the band, things were about to get worse. Both of Procol Harum's last two 1970s albums were compromised by their producers.

On paper, it might have looked like a dream opportunity for Brooker to work with his childhood heroes Leiber and Stoller (whose 'Poison Ivy' he'd recorded as the first Paramounts single). Just as the *Home* sessions had forged links back to Brooker's love of R&B, so Leiber and Stoller would forge links back to his love of soul. As producers, they'd steered a band as wayward as Stealers Wheel to success in 1972. The possibility must have seemed tempting that the pair could do the same for Procol Harum. And, amazingly, they did. 'Pandora's Box' soared to number 16 in the UK. But that triumph came with a lot of pain.

The difficulties began when the band repeated the *Home* habit of playing covers in the studio to loosen up. Brooker remembered it for *Goldmine* in 2010: 'Every day we'd go in and do a Leiber and Stoller song that we liked. I remember one day we went in and played 'Baby I Don't Care', which I think Elvis did. And they said, 'Gee guys, that's the best version we ever heard of that''. One side was playing the other, and I suspect it was the producers. A little nudge here and there, and all of a sudden, the producers had convinced the band to start *recording* some of these covers. And then they were recording a whole *album* of these covers. Brooker continued: 'They weren't interested in us doing just any covers. They wanted us to do a load of Peggy Lee songs. What we really should have been making was a Procol Harum album'. He elaborated for *Prog* in 2018: 'We had a constant battle with them because they had a catalogue of new songs that they wanted us to record. It was all very disruptive. And after we'd recorded most of the album, we finally got to do a Leiber and Stoller song'.

'I Keep Forgetting' wasn't just a Leiber and Stoller song but a *second-hand* one. Nor was it the only interloper. *Procol's Ninth* also included a cover of

The Beatles' 'Eight Days A Week'. Brooker told *Goldmine* in 2010: 'It puzzles me to this day how the other cover got in there. I think we just got fed up playing Leiber and Stoller songs to them when we got in the studio and just played a Beatles one. And they said, 'Hey, let's put that down!' and we put it down, and they put it down, and it ended up on the album'. In all this process of putting down, did nobody step in to say that, actually, this wasn't what the band was all about?

These bizarre decisions aside, Leiber and Stoller did the best they could with the new Procol Harum songs. Every piece was tightened to fighting fit. The production sparkles. The brass works well to differentiate the album as a new sound for a band still capable of progression. The very presence of these legends caused *Rolling Stone* to soften its abuse for a change, though the review was careful to praise the producers over the band:

> Despite the symphonic allusion in the title, *Procol's Ninth* is the hardest, grittiest recording the band has made in years. Wonderfully deft production and exceptional performances by B. J. Wilson (one of rock's best drummers), singer Gary Brooker and a newer member – guitarist Mick Grabham – make up for the often-deficient material. Lyricist Keith Reid has become Procol's weakest link. The two producers have also generously provided Procol with the best song on the album in 'I Keep Forgetting', which they wrote for Chuck Jackson in the early '60s. The track works so well that Procol might consider devoting an entire album to the works of Leiber/Stoller while sending Keith Reid on an extended leave of absence.

Rolling Stone was right about the material. Even Brooker later admitted that some of the songs weren't very good (and lack of material is surely *not* the truth of these sessions, is it?). But it was something of a circular argument. 'I Keep Forgetting' worked so well because the producers had a vested interest in making it work. What it overshadowed was an album full of songs by a band that had built its reputation and listener base on original material but which weren't quite the agenda the producers had brought to the sessions.

The single charted, and the album did good business on the back of it. But just look at how perfunctory it seems, how weary. *Procol's Ninth* was a dull title. The classical reference was cringe-inducing, especially for a band that had just avowed itself rid of its pretensions. And the cover was uninspired. Adding fake autographs might have seemed like a connection, except it wasn't. On one hand, it was a prideful artist signing their work, but on the other it was an artist who couldn't even be bothered to do it for real. Signed albums are special. *Procol's Ninth* was ordinary masquerading as premium. And the photo the signatures helped obscure looked a lot like school detention class. Wilson alone is smirking. The others have the expression of kids just told by the headmaster that their parents will have to be informed.

ort>8ort>8ort>8ffort>8ffort>8ffort>8ffort>8ffort>8ort>8ort>8ort>8ort>8ort>8ffort>8ffort>8ffort>8ort>8ort>8ort>8ort>8ort>8ffort>8ffort>8fffffort>8fort>8ort>8ort>8ort>8ort>8ort>8ort>8ort>8ort>8ort>8ort>8t>8t>8t>8t>8rt>8rt>8rt>8t>8t>8t>8t>8rt>8rt>8ffffort>8rt>8rt>8rt>8rt>8ort>8ort>8ort>8ort>8ort>8t>8t>8t>8t>8t>8t>8t>8t>8t>8**'Pandora's Box'** (Brooker, Reid)

Like 'Monsieur R. Monde' on *Exotic Birds And Fruit*, this repurposed 1967 song suggests a lack of new quality material. While we don't have a completed original version to tell us whether or not the words are new, they *do* sound like early Reid. In an effusive and seemingly random jumble, we meet Snow White, Pegasus, Handel, Cock Robin, a Persian that might be a cat, and more. The chorus wantonly mixes pirates in the Spanish Main (bringing 'Conquistador' to mind) with an Arabian magic carpet on some undisclosed quest to a 'marble staircased plain': possibly an Aztec temple. The notable thing that isn't mentioned is the title.

It's great to hear vintage Reid – even apparently meaningless vintage Reid – especially when allied to such a great production. Lieber and Stoller expertly crafted a slinky soundscape of marimba, synthesiser washes, flute, and Leslie-speaker guitar around Brooker's melody, flavouring one of the best Procol Harum tracks in ages. Brooker certainly thought so, enthusing to *Prog* in 2018: 'The best thing they did was 'Pandora's Box', which had strange instrumentation with a marimba. The way they had drawn out the instruments and made them weave in and out of each other was magnificent'.

The marimba isn't so strange when you remember that this is the band's third use of the instrument, but the flute is unique and something of a mystery, having been overdubbed in final, undocumented sessions in an unidentified studio in New York. An old reject the song might have been, but the production lifted it enough to score the much-needed hit, which in turn pulled the album at least partly up the charts in both the UK and US.

'Fool's Gold' (Brooker, Reid)

Up to 3:25, this is an attractive piano ballad with massive band choruses and chunky guitar breaks. But it really takes off in the fade when the producers introduce an understated brass counterpoint. The production and mix are again superb, highlighting Brooker's rough singing. But Reid's words are the same mordant self-reflection we're familiar with from songs like 'The Idol' on *Exotic Birds And Fruit*. He tried to be a hero doing his best, but he was deceived and ended up with nothing but a 'broken promise, empty lie'.

'Taking The Time' (Brooker, Reid)

Something of a restatement of the prior song, 'Taking The Time' isn't an ode to the joys of indolence, as you'd expect it to be, but a lament for the frustrations of indecision. Reid's narrator – whom it's hard to feel much sympathy for – complains that he's been 'living for the moment but the moment never came' and is instead ticking over, waiting for the world to come to *him* with a path forward. It's hard not to hear lines like 'Taking notes and stealing quotes/ Trying to make a name' as autobiography – a poet whose pursuit of success masks inner emptiness and whose retreat into domesticity can't dispel the growing suspicion that he hasn't actually achieved anything for himself. Reid did talk of his plans to write plays, movies, or a novel, but the only substantial written work we ever had from him was *My Own Choice* (2000): a limited-edition hardback selecting his favourites from his lyrics. There's been nothing more grandiose or substantial to date, though there's hope his papers might reveal some posthumous treasure: a pirate odyssey, say.

If any of that paragraph reminds you of John Lennon's 'Watching The Wheels', then there's also something coincidentally Lennon-esque about the music and performance Brooker chose for the song: a rock-'n'-roll ballad with blasts of despairing band chords. Again, the production enlivens it with sultry woodwinds and brass, adding a little self-deprecating jazz swagger like an unsympathetic commentary from just offstage.

'The Unquiet Zone' (Brooker, Reid)

The surprising production touch here is a funky Clavinet, dating the song to that specific moment in time when the instrument flavoured everything from Stevie Wonder's 'Superstition' to Pink Floyd's 'Shine On You Crazy Diamond'. It's mic'ed in stereo, immersing the listener in an instantly infectious rhythm. Immaculate horn stabs, Wilson's exuberant cowbell (his kit is also beautifully reproduced in stereo) and a fine Grabham solo help convert the mundane melody into one of the album's greatest pleasures.

But any hope that this might also be a surprise hit were stymied not by the subject itself (the horror of World War I trenches) – which might have been acceptable – but by lines like 'An awful waste of guts and gore' that Brooker enunciates clearly in gaps between the instruments. It's one thing to be told that war is wrong and to buy the song in solidarity with the cause of peace, but it's another to be shown just how bad it can be. By co-opting black music to this degree, Procol Harum showed an unbecoming blindness to bloody struggles much closer to their own time.

'The Final Thrust' (Brooker, Reid)

There's also something off-putting about the side one closer, which complicates its bouncy bass rhythm with syncopated ska guitar accents (softening us up for the all-out reggae on 'Without A Doubt') and then slaps Wilson's military drumming and more of those synth pads over the top. All of this only further disorientates the listener, who also has to negotiate Brooker's classical piano solos and a chorus that seems grafted on from a different song altogether. Reid seems to have tried to write an anthem for the masses, but his strident calls to get up and keep fighting, sit awkwardly against 'The Unquiet Zone', and you certainly won't be hearing *this* sung at the front, in picket lines, or on protest marches.

'I Keep Forgetting' (Leiber, Stoller)

Two cover versions bookend side two, the only two ever to appear on a Procol Harum studio album. This 1962 Leiber/Stoller composition (more correctly, 'I Keep Forgettin'') is here given a contemporary mix steeped in saxophones. It sounds great, and Brooker's vocal is terrifically framed, suggesting just how good the *Home* cover sessions could have been if a little more care had been taken in their polish. In retrospect, it's a shame the producers weren't given *those* tapes to work their dazzle on. It's also such a relief to have a song of heartbreak that doesn't twist the focus back to the songwriter's glum-faced egotism.

'Without A Doubt' (Brooker, Reid)
Given that 'Taking The Time' wanted us to be sympathetic to Reid for making nothing of his life, it was a little rich of him to stand up here and tell us all the things he'd achieve if only *something* didn't stand in his way. But the song makes it clear that the *something* is Reid himself, as attempts to realise any of the fabulous work of which he declares he's capable are sabotaged by his own inability to get going. He claims to have 'a great idea' for a deathless sonnet or a commercial book or play but can't decide on the first line. And yet, the block, in this case, somehow *did* result in a lyric, and a good one at that, so it's not an entirely convincing argument. All writers have good days and impossible days. Making a good day out of an impossible day is the mark of a professional, so Reid should be a lot happier than he looks.

Brooker coddled the words in a pleasing, upbeat song, diverting the band into reggae for part of the verses, and the producers worked all kinds of magic on the results, including slapping on a brass section. But the track is piecemeal and disjointed, fidgeting around for four minutes without ever getting comfortable or giving the listener a handle on what its creators are trying to say.

'The Piper's Tune' (Brooker, Reid)
This lyric is either a sustained volley of spite about some enemy's transgression or yet more self-recrimination. Though, if transgression is the case, 'You'll get no sweeties anymore' is hardly up to 'Simple Sister' levels of vitriol. Here is an apparent child (one that 'caused your mother great distress') who will now be punished, first by having no friends to play with and then by being skinned, hacked up and discarded. The actual transgression is never mentioned, only that it's 'a nasty mess' and an 'awful crime'. The title refers to the proverb 'He who pays the piper, calls the tune', but Reid seemingly misreads this as a synonym for 'You made your bed, now lie in it'. If the song is a mirror, then it may be a highly veiled attack on someone in the band, past or present, or an acknowledgement of how fragile his own talent was, as exposed in the previous track.

The song cries out for a ferocious sonic onslaught like 'Still There'll Be More', but, perversely, Brooker chose to drench it in Scottish idioms, including organ lines sounding like bagpipes. In 1976, he told *Street Life* that he couldn't understand why people didn't get his musical depth:

'The title would suggest what is actually the case: that there's a pibroch arrangement and pipe-band drumming. I don't recall reading anything about that. Perhaps the experiment wasn't successful, but somebody might have drawn attention to it'.

Maybe it's because commentators didn't know quite what to make of it. Chrysalis labelmates Jethro Tull had already used real bagpipes successfully on 'The Third Hoorah' on *War Child* (1974) and later created a creditable heavy metal pibroch on *Songs From The Wood*. Brooker's attempt comes across as either insincere pastiche or silly affectation, and without knowing which, it was probably easier for reviewers simply to ignore the piece altogether.

'Typewriter Torment' (Brooker, Reid)

Following on from the discussion in 'Without A Doubt', a true writer is compelled to write: it's built into their psyche. So this song must be heartfelt for Reid to even acknowledge the condition despite claiming it was just a piece of humour. For sure, there's some light-hearted wit involved. 'It eats up your life like a dose of the clap', he quips, a link back to the pencil that inspired 'A Souvenir Of London'. The song's twist is that his doctor won't give him a cure for the simple reason that writing makes money, and money pays the quack. So, by association, Reid is unable to break out of the lyric-writing business because lyrics are his cash cow, even if he could commit himself to those more risky artistic forms of self-expression he mentioned in 'Without A Doubt'.

This is another song that cried out for a muscular approach, but again, we didn't get it. There are lots of Grabham guitars but no solos, the tempo is moribund and Brooker's tune is nothing special. Leiber and Stoller did all they could to smother the track in stereo tricks, but even layers of percussive overdubs couldn't make it zing.

'Eight Days A Week' (Lennon, McCartney)

This throwaway recording might have been intended as a rebuke to the producers, but it's actually a lot of fun. You can understand why Leiber and Stoller put on the album: to counteract the sedate rhythms and predictable arrangements of the Brooker/Reid songs, let alone all that lyric negativity. Brooker's soaring and soulful rendition gives the song the same reverence as when he sang his favourite songs in the *Home* cover-version sessions, and he genuinely delights in the jumpy rhythm. It's the only track where everybody in the studio seems to be enjoying themselves.

'The Adagio D'Albinoni' (1976)

Personnel:
Gary Brooker: piano
Alan Cartwright: acoustic bass
Chris Copping: organ
Mick Grabham: guitar
B.J. Wilson: drums
Written by: Giazotto (arranged by Procol Harum)
Recorded: 1976, Shepperton Film Studios, London, UK
Producer: Procol Harum
Label: Chrysalis
Release date: 1976 (France)
Charts: did not chart
Length: 6:06

Little is documented about this France-only single. It's hardly obscure but has barely made it onto any expanded CD editions. The A-side has been released as a bonus track once on the Friday Music version of *Procol's Ninth* (2005) and was anthologised only on *A&B – The Singles* (2002), which evidently was put together with access to the master tapes but didn't want to tell us anything about its creation. Neither of the band's big boxes (*All This And More...* and *Still There'll Be More*) felt fit to include it. There's even uncertainty about the title – listed as 'Adagio Di Albinoni' on the picture sleeve only – and the piece itself wasn't even written by Tomaso Albinoni in the 17th century but by Remo Giazotto in 1958. The nearest thing we have to a true title in English is 'Adagio In G Minor, For Strings And Organ, On Two Thematic Ideas And On A Figured Bass By Tomaso Albinoni'.

Procol Harum's links to the piece are sketchy simply because we have no official record of them actually playing it in the 1970s, though it had been hanging around for a while. Copping attempted a solo rendition with orchestra at Edmonton in 1972, which never made it to a release of *Procol Harum Live* and was apparently a disaster. The band finally pieced together a band arrangement for a tour of France in 1975, as a result of which Chrysalis decided it might make a good single there. It was duly recorded with a mobile studio. But the length and style weren't suitable for rock radio, and it didn't seem to interest French buyers. Another glum photo didn't help, though it does include Keith Reid.

Prog rock fans will know the composition from Renaissance's 'Cold Is Being' on *Turn Of The Cards* (1974), to which Betty Thatcher added lyrics and where Michael Dunford claimed authorship of the music. Procol Harum play their instrumental with solemn sincerity, to begin with, but they increasingly allow Grabham to solo and Wilson to thrash around without once summoning enough spirit to give the thing legs. For sure, there's a thematic and sonic link to 'A Whiter Shade Of Pale', which means this couldn't be any other band, but neither does it have a spark of excitement nor – on this reading at least – enthusiasm among its players.

'The Blue Danube' (Strauss)

The B-side has reached a significantly wider audience, as it's actually an uncredited live performance from Bournemouth Winter Gardens on 17 March 1976, and was included in full on *All This And More...*, and also along with the rest of D.I.R. Broadcasting's 53-minute *British Biscuit* recording of that gig on *Still There'll Be More*. Moreover, we have a number of other live recordings of 'The Blue Danube' from the period, stand-alone and incorporated into the middle of 'Grand Hotel'. It was mainly played live for laughs, but it does pack a visceral punch when Grabham roars in on guitar, and it's one of the better of those types of amped-up classical arrangements with anthemic guitar that British prog-rock band The Enid soon made their own.

The released single contains a highly edited version of the original performance (from 8:09 down to 6:25), omitting the introduction and solo piano section, but it does leave in the applause and is significantly better than the A-side. The band are delighted with their ability to negotiate the piece's deceptive complexity, and the audience screams encouragement at each restatement of a piece that most of them knew best from taking drugs while watching *2001: A Space Odyssey*. There's even someone who has fun with a whistle.

Evidently, the band also recorded a version of the piece at Abbey Road in 1975 for the compilation album *In Strauss Und Bogen,* released in Austria to celebrate 150 years since the birth of Johann Strauss. Before performing the piece at Leicester University on 29 November 1975 (heard on the 2018 Esoteric Recordings edition of *Procol's Ninth*), Brooker told the audience about its creation: 'We got a strange request from Vienna. They said, 'Would you like to be part of an album and play 'The Blue Danube'?'. So we said, 'Not our bag, but we'll give it a try'. And we gave it a try, and it ended up in dire straits'. That one *is* righteously obscure. I've never heard it. The 2004 Friday Music version of *Exotic Birds And Fruit* claimed to have it, but that's actually just the Bournemouth Winter Gardens B-side. *In Strauss Und Bogen* must be a different performance since it was released (and Brooker mentioned it) months before the band played Bournemouth. And yet, to date, nobody's come up with the evidence.

Something Magic (1977)

Personnel:
Gary Brooker: piano, vocals
Chris Copping: bass
Mick Grabham: guitars
Pete Solley: keyboards
Barrie Wilson: drums
Recorded: 1976, Criteria Studios, Miami, USA
Producers: Procol Harum, Ron Albert, Howard Albert
Label: Chrysalis
Release date: February 1977
Charts: US: 147
Running time: 40:30 (A: 21:52, B: 18:38)

A little strife in the studio was acceptable if the results were hit songs and press respectability. Procol Harum might have been happy to work again with Leiber and Stoller on what became *Something Magic*, but the pair turned them down. The producers' preoccupation with Elkie Brooks gets the blame, but that doesn't seem likely. Accounts are murky, with Brooker at various times saying the band were keen to work with the producers again but had no intention of doing so. Eventually, they chose a different pair of American producers. Howard and Ron Albert had worked to Americanise Curved Air (*Midnight Wire*) and Wishbone Ash (*New England*). They should have been a good match. But the pair's relationship with Procol Harum was fraught and short-lived. Brooker told *Record Collector* in 1995:

> We went to Criteria Studios in Florida, which was producing all the good sounds at the time, like The Eagles and The Bee Gees. So we played our 16 songs to the producers, these two brothers, Ron and Howie Albert. We went back into the control room, and they said, 'Well, what do you want us to do?'. So I said, 'We want you to engineer'. Silence. Then they said, 'Well, you know, you can take a dog shit and cover it in chocolate, but when you bite into it, what have you got? Dog shit!'.

Booker told *Prog* in 2018: 'We should have gone home then. I think we were shocked more than anything. If we'd been more mercenary and sensible, we would have turned 'round and said, 'You guys can fuck off too'. They said shortly after that, 'We wouldn't even be here, but our boat's broken'. In the end, it was a co-production, so we weren't doing everything they'd say'. This ambiguity, that the Albert brothers were producers, engineers, co-producers, or just sitting there bored in the studio racking up fees for their boat, extended into the music itself, which Brooker claimed was largely directed by the band. He laid out the rationale for its creation for *New Musical Express* in 1977: 'We realised we were going into the studios with all the ideas, and very often the ideas were just being blocked or changed, because that was what a producer was meant to do. Really, the albums weren't coming out how we wanted them. We'd made nine albums, and obviously, we knew enough about it to be able to go in and sort it out. Which is what we did'.

But elsewhere, there's the strong suggestion that the band auditioned all their material for the Albert brothers, and it was *they* who chose what was to be recorded. Equally in doubt is the thinking behind the new studio and the new ears. In 1976, Procol Harum were desperate to update their sound to chase the AOR market that had seen them rapidly eclipsed by younger, smoother, more radio-friendly bands with big, bold, anthemic productions. The shock success of the American band Boston was on everybody's minds that year. Procol Harum could have been another British act that crossed the Atlantic to vast acclaim, like Fleetwood Mac or Al Stewart. They had a style that could easily have been adapted for hits with a big showy production: the *Grand Hotel* sumptuousness splashed across a new canvas. They could even have been the next Robin Trower. And yet they chose to fill half the album with 'The Worm And The Tree', a spoken-word conceptual piece.

Some of this calculation *might* have made sense. Brooker had recently played synthesizer on an all-star prog-rock version of *Peter And The Wolf* narrated by Vivian Stanshall, which was artistically brilliant even if it was commercially dead. One side songs and one side an extended piece was actually the format Procol Harum had employed on their biggest success to date, *Procol Harum Live*. It was the best of both worlds: commercial blockbusters for new kids and a little prog for the old fans. What they forgot – and what the Albert brothers seemed acutely aware of – was that they wouldn't have anything at all if the songs weren't strong. And they weren't. Moreover, the market for grand prog gestures was in a perilous state by 1976, let alone the following year when the album was released. A very small, select group of artists with huge audiences could carry side-length or near-side-length epics in this troublesome time. Pink Floyd, Yes, and Emerson, Lake & Palmer all managed it. But Procol Harum didn't have anything like the same fan base.

You'd suppose the Albert brothers might have nixed the pretensions straight away, particularly if the band really did have 16 songs to record. Brooker maintains the brothers *were* interested in the piece, rather than simply having given up on the band and therefore been happy to wrap up a lost cause with a side that could be recorded in a day, but there's also the same ambiguity. Brooker told *New Musical Express* in 1977: 'When we went in there, it could have turned out to be like *Exotic Birds* or *Ninth*. We didn't even know we were going to do 'The Worm'. We just played it one morning. Nobody knew it, and it was very much improvised on the spot. Whereas, if you go in with producers, after six weeks, you end up doing only the numbers you told them about on the very first day. But I think we're more aware of what the songs are like and how they should sound. So, because we were producing, this album is much more what we're like'.

In 1977, Brooker told *Rock Around The World*: 'The last two albums were more presentations of just a package of songs. There wasn't a big song there. We'd gone for that, for a simple rock format, but it didn't go down that well with the record-buying public, so we thought we'd have a go at putting a big one on this album: a bit more of a chance'. It's hard to follow that chain of reasoning, except that Procol Harum were batted around like a pinball, from one failed experiment to another, heedless of the understanding that constantly revising your sound might be exacerbating the failure. The last thing they needed was a change in personnel, but Alan Cartwright was out in June 1976 after one too many arguments with Grabham. Copping shifted back to bass, and new keyboard player Pete Solley was drafted in. His synth-playing updated the band's live style and attempted a little continuity with the sound for which, a decade on, they were still remembered best. Prog-rock fans will know Solley as a member of British band Paladin, but when Solley got the call, he'd been working most prominently in the band Snafu alongside Procol Harum member from way back when: Bobby Harrison!

Not the last-minute change, the frantic attempt to update their sound, nor even the excellent mysterious cover painting by *Procol Harum Live* artist Bruce Meek could save the band from the downward spiral that, in retrospect, they seem to have experienced since *Procol Harum Live* at least (or since the first single if you want to be brutal). Though it's usual to pin the blame on punk, *that* was wholly irrelevant. Procol Harum had shifted their market back to America for *Something Magic*, and America had little interest in punk when the airwaves were filled with corporate-rock acts for young adults and a buoyant dance craze for the kids. America didn't want Procol Harum, so that was that. Within months of the album's release, the band that had soldiered on so doggedly for all these years finally collapsed. All that punk achieved in the UK was to lob empty cans at the wreck of the band's hopes, lying there rusted and worthless on the side of the road.

'Something Magic' (Brooker, Reid)
After half a minute of shrill string-dominated chords reminiscent of 'Tell All The People' by The Doors, this big production settles into a piano riff and Booker's fine melody, to which the band respond with dramatic guitar stabs and thunderous drumming over which the producers craft manic orchestral flourishes. A startling woodwind feature sounds like a crazed refraction of David Bowie's 'Moonage Daydream', while the strings have much in common with Electric Light Orchestra's magnificently wayward *Eldorado*.

These are not flippant references. The song was constructed to hit all those cultural beats and more. It's so thoroughly overblown that it could easily seem like parody, yet 'Something Magic' is merely the culmination of all the band's classical aspirations since 1967 (a close cousin to the 1972 'Conquistador' or 'Grand Hotel'), except it's as if we've suddenly wrenched the band from its Procol Harum bubble and into a world in which The Doors,

David Bowie, ELO, and many others are crowding for the same outrageous sonic space. An irresistible three minutes and a blatantly calculated hit single, it's mystifying that Chrysalis ignored this song. They even threw it away on the B-side of 'Wizard Man' in the US. It could have caught fire in this same era as Manfred Mann's Earth Band's 'Blinded By The Light', not to mention Steve Miller's *Book Of Dreams*, Yes' *Going For The One* and Meat Loaf's all-conquering *Bat Out Of Hell*.

Let's briefly remind ourselves that there *is* a lyric, too, and it's not at all as mordant as we're used to. Indeed, 'Something magic being born' is almost as upbeat as a chorus cry. Sure, Reid's words are just a catalogue of horror-movie tropes (drunkards, demons, vultures, along with his usual insipient storms), but there are chinks of sunlight between the night terrors, and it's fascinating to speculate on what bizarre process led from Brooker's initial jumpy, film-noir-style treatment to the finished track's outpouring of multitracked extravagance.

'Skating On Thin Ice' (Brooker, Reid)
Having exhausted the listener, it was imperative that the album give space to breathe. With that in mind, 'Skating On Thin Ice' is an enchanting, soft ballad bedded on one of Brooker's favourite compositional styles, the classical waltz. In a 1970 Australian TV documentary (see the 'Beyond These Things' chapter at the end of the book), Copping had teased that he might eventually move into songwriting, but this is the most we ever got from him – an arrangement for orchestra and uncredited female voices onto which are grafted wildly inappropriate whooshing skate effects. Reid is back in self-pitying mode, but for the second time, you'll hardly notice his words.

'Wizard Man' (Brooker, Reid)
In the book of rules for perfectly sequenced 1970s pop albums, we ought to be pulled to our feet with another rocker, and that's exactly what this track provides. Oddly, it doesn't seem to have been meant to be here, having been left off the tracklisting on the UK and European cover – it appears only on the label. The US version *did* list it, but the lyric was omitted from the inner sleeve. A last-minute decision or not, the idea was again blatant: give the album something simple and commercial that radio could play. Brooker told *Rock Around The World* in 1977: 'I think 'Wizard Man' is probably the only one we've done that on. It's the only one that we thought in the studio, 'This is a single, we'll make it as such".

It's short, upbeat, and in a style of heartland soft rock that was guaranteed to slot it into FM radio programming. There's a catchy melody and an inoffensive lyric. Everything's right. But it failed in the market. You can well imagine Brooker throwing his hands up in despair. Evidently, nothing was going to rescue the band, not even a surefire smash. So, what was the point in carrying on?

'The Mark Of The Claw' (Grabham, Reid)
Grabham had already written a number of songs for Cochise, so he decided
he'd like a Trower-style slice of Procol Harum's songwriting pie. Reid gave
him a set of his most daunting words to craft into something acceptable.
The lyric consists merely of sentence fragments that reprise 'Lime Street
Blues' (and through that, Bob Dylan's 'Percy's Song') to chronicle a police
investigation into what appears to be a fatal car crash. Was it premeditated?
To quote Frank Zappa's contemporaneous courtroom parody 'The Illinois
Enema Bandit', the verdict is 'Let the fiend go free'. There's no comprehensible
connection to the title, which seems to link the song again to film noir and
horror-movie motifs. Reid told *Zigzag* in 1977: 'I have a standard which I've
set myself, and it's important for me to progress as a writer. If you look at the
lyric of 'The Mark Of The Claw', there is no one else who could have written
that, whereas I was certainly fairly heavily influenced on the first album. Just
to maintain that thing of being original is difficult'.

Grabham's response was a blend of piano ballad with melodramatic guitar
chords, to which the Albert brothers added a cornucopia of sound effects and
Solley's time-capsule analogue synthesizer solo. There's a lot to unpack in the
song, but it's likely few fans have ever taken the time to do so and have simply
seen it as an over-fussy wrapping around a too-brief Grabham guitar workout.

'Strangers In Space' (Brooker, Reid)
The song side's finale is its longest and least-engaging track. It's 6:03 of
muggy synths, chiming Fender Rhodes, and becalmed blues like we're back
on that glassy ocean at the start of 'Whaling Stories'. Brooker pitches his
melody outside his usual range, attempting to breathe life into a bleak Reid
lyric where the phrase 'Something uncovered, something unsaid' seems to
directly rebuke the positivity of 'Something Magic' all those minutes ago.

'The Worm And The Tree' (Brooker, Reid)
A band that had once resisted putting lyrics along with their albums now
devoted a gatefold inner spread to Reid's libretto for this side-length
composition, presenting it as the album's centrepiece and as a career
masterpiece. There are seven densely-written six-line stanzas, all in the
same rigid anapaestic tetrameter – the same singsong rhythm often used
in children's verse (Dr. Seuss used it for *The Cat In The Hat*) and jaunty,
galloping heroic fables. They tell the saga of 'a great tree' that becomes
infected by 'a small worm'. Each day, the worm eats a little more of the tree,
and each day, the tree grows a little weaker. Soon the rest of the forest has
shrunk away in disgust from the infected tree, fearful of sharing its fate,
and the tree becomes 'loathsome' and noxious to the extent that it begins to
poison the local animals. A young man comes to the rescue, chopping down
the tree and burning it to ash, worm and all. You've got to kill to cure, Reid
concludes, but eventually, a new tree will grow in its place.

It's a fun little parable, poised between Eric Carle's *The Very Hungry Caterpillar* (1969) and early Rupert Bear stories, which could be gothic, scary and moralistic. Reid could have marketed it as an illustrated book, but the fairy-tale style is so anachronistic that it would have been hard to sell to a publisher in the 1970s, and readers might have been put off by the lack of character or strong story beats. There's also an excruciating pun on 'elder' in the last line, conveniently glossing over the fact that the elder is one of the weediest and least attractive of British hedgerow plants: hardly the majestic shapely tree the story describes. Still, those are deficiencies a good painter could correct, and visually, the idea of a huge tree becoming progressively more monstrous might lend itself to fine treatment at the hands of illustrators like Stephen Gammell or Edward Gorey. It could have worked. But as a pop album side, that's more of a gamble, even in the year of Bob Johnson and Peter Knight's *The King Of Elfland's Daughter* and with *Jeff Wayne's Musical Version Of The War Of The Worlds* (with which it shares some similarities) in production.

Reid claimed it was always intended as a Procol Harum lyric. He explained to *Zigzag* in 1977:

The idea for it came about a few years ago. People had been asking when we were going to do another extended thing like 'In Held', and I also felt it would be nice to have something like that to do onstage. So I thought about it, and it seemed that when people do things like that, they tend to make them overcomplicated. So it struck me that it would be better to do something really straightforward and let everything else around it be more complicated. I wanted the storyline to be very simple so that there would be lots of room for descriptive music.

It certainly *is* a simple story, but Reid maintained there was a hidden twist in the tale. He told *New Musical Express* in 1977: 'Really, it's about how the press nearly caused the band to break up. That was three years ago, but we've been on the point of disbanding many times'.

So the tree is Procol Harum, the worm is the music press (though 'Butterfly Boys', recorded three years prior, suggests it might also signify Chrysalis), and the young man...is what? Brooker or Reid deciding to destroy Procol Harum? A band that had grown diseased and unmarketable? The killing-off of an old style of music exemplified by 'A Whiter Shade Of Pale' that had infected the band and all those around it? The disease surely wasn't classical rock since that's exactly the medium Brooker used to present the tale. He told *Prog* in 2018:

Keith Reid had written a long story called 'The Worm And The Tree', and I'd always envisaged it as being fairytale-like with melodies and instruments depicting the characters. So I played it to them (the Albert brothers), and they said, 'That's interesting'. I'd not thought about singing it, and it ended up being spoken. So I orchestrated it and we got a few guys in playing strings and woodwinds, beefing it up. Suddenly, after ten years, and with our tenth album, we have another 18-minute piece. We'd gone full circle. And when you were looking around comparing that with what else was going on, you thought, 'Wait a minute, we might have lost touch here'.

The idea that the piece should be recited seems to have been mostly for expediency since Brooker was unable to come up with a tune to suit all those thumping triplets. Both Brooker and Reid told interviewers that they wanted to bring in an outside narrator, such as James Mason. But in the end, Brooker recited the text himself, which solved the problem within the tight timescales in which the piece was developed and recorded but ruined its chances of being received well by fans or of having much lasting respect in the prog community. The general disdain with which 'The Worm And The Tree' is viewed means that there weren't howls of protest in 2009 when the Salvo edition of *Something Magic* managed to edit the piece by almost two minutes without advertising the fact. If you have the Salvo CD, you might not even know it's incomplete. Despite that beautiful inner gatefold, there wasn't much care in the presentation, with various labels and releases undecided about whether the title should have an ampersand.

The piece is in three distinct blocks separated by long silences: 'Part One', 'Two' and 'Three'. These are, in turn, subdivided into eight named sections, each one but 'Battle' consisting of a musical sequence followed by or incorporating a verse, and each in turn separated by shorter silences. They're beautiful in composition and production, from the resplendent solo grand piano that opens the suite to Brooker's masterful orchestration, subtly interwoven with the band at its most stately. A much more measured, careful and sophisticated approach to classical rock than anything on *Procol Harum Live*, 'The Worm And The Tree' contains moments of grandeur that ought to impress even the most jaded prog-rock survivor, with none of the cloying over-arrangement that so often weighs down works by Renaissance and the like. Subtle touches such as Grabham's string bending to represent the worm in 'Menace', and Solley's synthesizer to personify the young man in 'Enervation', are deftly handled, while 'Battle' gave Grabham the chance for an extended solo against whirls of strings: his career peak.

But the narration *is* a problem, even though the Albert brothers drenched it in reverb to make it sound like Brooker was proclaiming from a concert stage (an effect similar to the one on Rick Wakeman's 1974 live hit album *Journey To The Centre Of The Earth*, narrated by David Hemmings, which had proved itself acceptable to listeners). Brooker is not a bad talker, and he does the best with the material. His voice is flavoursome and warm, sounding a great deal like Mike Pinder's recitations on Moody Blues albums. But Reid's starchy words give him little chance to emote. The piece is hamstrung from the first awkward line: 'Into a great tree a small worm did go'. It's surprising that

Esoteric Recordings or another label hasn't yet released an instrumental-only version, which might finally enable a more positive re-evaluation.

'Backgammon' (Brooker)
The B-side of the UK 'Wizard Man' single was Brooker's only solo writing credit to that date. A funky R&B instrumental, it builds to attractive Grabham phrases mixed with Solley's most overt synth noises. But there's nothing that's distinctively Procol Harum and the whole point seems to be merely to occupy the time, a bit like the way the band took to fending off boredom when touring by playing actual backgammon. Moreover, the song title is a reference to the Booker T. & The M.G'.s track 'Chinese Checkers' (1965), a piece to which this castoff is an uncomfortably close cousin.

The Prodigal Stranger (1991)

Personnel:
Gary Brooker: piano, acoustic guitar, vocals
Matthew Fisher: organ
Robin Trower: electric guitar
Dave Bronze: bass
Mark Brzezicki: drums
Jerry Stevenson: Spanish guitar, mandolin
Henry Spinetti: drums ('The Truth Won't Fade Away')
Steve Lange, Maggie Ryder, Miriam Stockley: vocals ('Holding On')
Recorded: 1989-1991, The Loft, Battery Studios, New York, USA; The Stone
Room, London; Black Barn, Surrey; Old Barn, South Croydon, UK
Producers: Matt Noble, Gary Brooker, Keith Reid, Matthew Fisher
Label: Zoo Entertainment
Release date: August 1991
Charts: did not chart
Running time: 51:53

Procol Harum were always Gary Brooker's band. That was surely true during their original run when personnel came and went, but he was always the dominant writer and singer. And it's self-evident about their many latter-day incarnations in which there was essentially one star onstage plus a supporting cast. Procol Harum were so intimately Brooker's conception that it's now impossible to imagine anybody else taking the singer's role. Even Keith Reid – as we learned with *Novum* – is subordinate.

The story of Procol Harum is, therefore, the story of what Brooker decided to do with the band, which for about 14 years was nothing at all. He launched a solo career in 1979, played for years with Eric Clapton, and played keyboards or sang on albums by Wings, The Hollies, George Harrison, and The Alan Parsons Project, among others. Brooker even wrote a ballet. In the downtime between Procol Harum projects, he continued touring with his own band or others, most notably as part of ensembles led by Ringo Starr and Bill Wyman, earning the ultimate accolade by playing Hammond organ on two Kate Bush albums. Though solo acclaim eluded Brooker, he always had enough recognition to enhance everything he touched and shifted effortlessly into a role as one of the elder statesmen of British rock. He likely could have achieved little of this without the cachet of 'A Whiter Shade Of Pale'. But with every year that passed, that song seemed less of a burden. It was generally played live and not as an obligation. Star power was such that it was always the song and the singer that were required for nostalgic satisfaction, not the band. So why resurrect Procol Harum at all?

It wasn't a given. After all, Brooker's third solo album *Echoes In The Night* (1985) included B. J. Wilson and Matthew Fisher among its players, and Reid wrote half its lyrics. Could Brooker have believed that the Procol Harum name would sell more? Could the press announcements have at least caused a few now-hopefully-mellow music journalists to prick up their ears? And most of all, as Brooker might have had little expectation of a hit single or big-selling album (and *The Prodigal Stranger* managed neither), could the album have been a platform for him to launch the Procol Harum concerts, which were always a lucrative event, and doubly so when an orchestra (well out of his means as a solo performer) was involved? In 1997, Brooker told the *Daily Express* that it all stemmed from a visit to Bill Wyman's restaurant Sticky Fingers:

> They had live radio going to America, and they had about six different radio stations with DJs broadcasting live from Sticky Fingers. And loads of rock stars go up there and chat on the radio and they play the records and all that. So I was invited up there, and I met lots of people, and they were all talking about the band as if it still existed and with a lot of respect. They were asking, 'When are we going to see the band again?'. So, afterwards, I thought, 'Well, people still like us and we haven't played for 15 years' or however long it was. I'd thought I was going to make a solo album, but then I said to Keith, 'What do you think about the Procol thing?'.

Reid had emigrated to America in the early 1980s and had largely given up writing lyrics, suffering what he called burnout. He'd only slowly started to write words for people other than Brooker and got back into the habit. He spoke to *The Chicago Tribune* shortly after the release of *The Prodigal Stranger* lead single 'All Our Dreams Are Sold' in August 1991:

> A couple of years ago, I got a phone call from Gary. He said, 'What about getting together and writing some songs and making a Procol Harum album?' And I said, 'Well, I'll tell you what. Get on a plane and come to New York and let's see if we can write some worthwhile songs'. So he came to New York a few days later, and we spent about ten days woodshedding and working on tunes. We had a lot of fun, and we came up with some good stuff. Then I went over to England, and we called up Matthew Fisher, our old organ player, and got together with him and wrote some songs, and they turned out well. Eventually, we started to feel we really had some worthwhile stuff, so let's maybe go ahead and make a record.

There was another more personal reason, as Brooker explained to *Progression* in 1996. It had to do with Wilson's 1987 drug overdose, likely a suicide bid, which left him in a coma: 'There was a hope he might come out of it if he knew what was going on. I spoke to Keith Reid about doing a new Procol Harum album. We wrote songs, and Matthew got involved and it just sort of grew organically. We sent the tapes with a drum machine on it to (Wilson). They put headphones on his head, but it didn't wake him up'.

Wilson never did wake up, not even to rant at being replaced by a hated machine and died in 1990. The album was dedicated to his memory.

Since leaving Procol Harum in 1969, Fisher's career had been patchy. His first solo album *Journey's End* didn't reach stores until 1973, and in the meantime, he'd been all but forgotten. There were no hits, and both *Journey's End* and its hastily recorded follow-up *I'll Be There* contained sour references to his old band: in particular, a dig at Brooker called 'Going For A Song', suggesting a scab he couldn't stop picking. When Brooker called him back to the band, it was a win for both men; since Fisher got another shot at the big time, Brooker gave his revived Procol Harum a little more credibility, and the hatchet was seemingly buried.

There was one more component to add to achieve the classic Procol Harum sound. In the interview CD that Zoo Entertainment shipped to radio stations on the album's release, Reid explained: 'The question of guitar obviously started to appear, and I think that we weren't sure whether Robin would be interested in working with us. But anyway, we took the tapes along and played them to him, and he loved it. In fact, he said, 'Why didn't you call me sooner?'. But there was a catch. Trower agreed to play on the album but bowed out of any live promotional work. Since his departure, Trower had become a blues-rock powerhouse, recording a number of well-received albums, though sales had slackened appreciably since the 1970s. This could be another kick up the charts. He told *Guitar* in 1993: 'I loved the songs, but in the end, there wasn't enough room for me to do my thing without ruining the songs, and I was wanting to get back to playing blues'.

Thus reconstituted, the band patched together *The Prodigal Stranger* over a long period in a large number of studios on both sides of the Atlantic. For the first time, it was a CD album: 12 tracks totalling 52 minutes. It certainly wasn't sequenced with vinyl in mind. Its producer, Matt Noble, had a prior association with Procol Harum, even if all but the most dedicated of fans wouldn't have recognized his name. He'd helped put together the earliest Brooker/Reid demos in 1966. Now, he fulfilled the same function, adding synthesized backing for many of the demos, in the process helping develop a few of the songs. Other players also came from past associations, such as bassist Dave Bronze and drummer Henry Spinetti, who'd both played on *Echoes In The Night*. Big Country drummer Mark Brzezicki and guitarist Jerry Stevenson were recommended for the project, the latter to fill out Trower's sound.

It sounded right: big and boxy and new. There were high hopes. But the album's failure stymied hopes for new recordings, at least in the near future. Brooker told UCLA Radio in 2001: 'We saw that as a bit of a start if you like. A new era. But it was a California record company Zoo Records that ended up putting that out, and they pulled the rug from under us. I don't think it made as much back as they'd put into the video (for 'The Truth Won't Fade Away'), which we didn't want done'.

In fact, *The Prodigal Stranger* simply suffered from bad timing. There *was* a market for heritage prog, but it wouldn't open up until later the same decade. In this case, being ahead of the curve was not an advantage. But Brooker was right to think there was a receptive audience just waiting for him, and better days lay ahead.

'The Truth Won't Fade Away' (Brooker, Reid, Fisher)
With its shiny pop production, pin-sharp snare drum and a gloss of synths, this opener sets out the stall for a Procol Harum that wasn't stuck in the past or targeted only at older fans. Brooker's voice has an attractive new quaver about it – a little reminiscent of David Byrne – and the melody soars. But Reid's lyric is self-reverential, like so many anthems by bands of earlier generations that were then touting themselves as the rebels of their age.

'Holding On' (Brooker, Reid)
Reid's criticism of religious warmongering is barbed, to say the least, because even though he references a range of conflicts – not all of which were driven by faith ('killing fields', for example) – the desert imagery of the first verse centres the song in the Middle East, and there are limited interpretations of the closing lines 'Religious leaders teaching hate/Praise the war and call it fate'. Neither are there answers, but simply the sloganeering of the title.

Much more fascinating is Brooker's treatment, which uses African rhythms, voices, and flavours to widen the song's scope. Brooker noted in the Zoo promotional CD: 'It was thrown somewhere towards Ethiopia, to the best of my recollection, and we needed some girls to do some chanting. And these girls came along and they were South Africans, and they were quite fluent in either Swahili or Zulu. I'm not sure what language it is, but they taught us all how to sing it, and it ended up interesting'.

It's all a little *too* worthy, even for that period when pop leapt on Africa as a means of showing it cared. But the chorus is triumphant, and Brooker gives it all the heart he has.

'Man With A Mission' (Brooker, Reid, Noble)
A swingbeat rhythm and fat shape-throwing synth sounds make this a litmus test for old and new listeners alike. Existing fans may think it the most excruciating thing in the band's catalogue, while Gen X's will curl their toes at dad rock trying to sound like the streets. But Brooker claims the style unashamedly, turning another slight Reid lyric into a celebration of independent thinking as if *daring* the kids to sneer.

'(You Can't) Turn Back The Page' (Brooker, Reid, Noble)
Recognising the danger of losing their fan base by piling on too many contemporary styles up front, Procol Harum here kick back for an unashamedly old-fashioned ballad. And though the dominant instrument is

synths rather than the grand piano and strings of the earlier band, there's still space for the classic Hammond sound. It's the prettiest melody on the album, and Brooker's voice has enough of his old flavour to win over the sceptical.

'One More Time' (Brooker, Reid, Fisher)

Since this features Trower, you won't be surprised to find it's a straightforward blues. The words are generic where-did-our-love-go pleading, and Trower's solos have none of his early ferocity. It's pleasant, but it's not special, and somehow, you'd expect more from Fisher's involvement, if only a little touch of classicism to enrich the changes.

'A Dream In Ev'ry Home' (Brooker, Reid, Fisher)

Fisher has much more to say here. He explained on the Zoo promotional CD: 'It was just a riff that I thought up at home. I sequenced it up on my computer, with a bass line and a drum part that no real bass player would ever have played or drummer would not have played. It's not what real musicians would have done'.

   In the studio, the band recreated the demo as an attractive ballad bedded on synths and piano and accented by more of the album's signature chorus of backing singers. It sounds gorgeous, which makes Reid's caustic lyric as bafflingly contrary as in the days of *Grand Hotel* or *Exotic Birds And Fruit*. He describes that ubiquitous box in our living rooms not just as a 'T.V. Ceasar' but as 'the hand that reached inside your purse'. And there's no real call for the apostrophe in the title.

'The Hand That Rocks The Cradle' (Brooker, Reid, Thompson)

Propelled by an infectious funk rhythm and Brooker's winning Peter Gabriel-style hollers, this mid-album highlight ups the tempo and the energy and brightens the mood appreciably. We already know that Brooker can sell even the most negative lyric, but here, at least, Reid gives him something positive to latch onto: a genuinely uplifting faith in the promise of better days.

'The King Of Hearts' (Brooker, Reid, Noble)

A deck of playing cards is an iconic image for Procol Harum, one that can only be used with the greatest solemnity. You don't back casually into a quote from 'A Whiter Shade Of Pale'. But on the Zoo promotional CD, Reid suggested that's exactly what he did: 'The genesis of that song is the actual line, 'The king of hearts': the king no longer being the king of hearts but the king of the broken-hearted. And then that took me on a little voyage. When we got to that point in the verse, the card game was going on, and the characters just seemed to speak out for themselves, and they started talking about wandering through their playing cards. So I just wrote it down'.

   Brooker refused to take the bait, instead constructing an arrangement of snakelike meandering through foggy midnight streets. There's the Hammond sound for sure and the same slow anthemic tempo, but it doesn't evoke 'Pale', particularly given Trower's blues-guitar interjections.

'All Our Dreams Are Sold' (Brooker, Reid, Trower)
Having damned the sly persuasions of television commercialism in 'A Dream In Ev'ry Home', it's a little redundant to provoke listeners with a *second* song about money on the same album. But get past the sermonising, and the song delivers exactly what we've been missing so far: five minutes of honest, high-wattage guitar-led rock 'n' roll. It doesn't matter that the song isn't very good or that Brooker phones in the melody and can't summon enthusiasm for the chorus. The song leaps out of the album, and Trower plays a couple of well-shaped solos that are almost transcendent. Zoo rightly thought the guitarist to be a recognisable-enough star to propel the song into the charts. It hit 29 in the US, a worthy placing for a band with Procol Harum's awkward baggage in a year dominated by the likes of Metallica and Nirvana.

'Perpetual Motion' (Brooker, Reid, Noble)
This is the only song on *The Prodigal Stranger* that could have been transplanted seamlessly into one of the band's mid-1970s albums, almost without changing a note or (save for the more modern technology) an instrument. It's Reid's best lyric on the album, merging more of those old tropes (sailing ships, basements, dancing, silken sheets) with Shakespearian references that hoist the mood out of the ordinary and into the unsteady states of the imagination he used to inhabit. Brooker responds dutifully with an elegant melody, and Fisher adds his most prominent organ feature on the album.

'Learn To Fly' (Brooker, Reid, Fisher)
This second Fisher demo, to which Reid added words and which was reworked in the studio, is far less successful than 'A Dream In Ev'ry Home'. The snappy tempo, American rock stylings and Reid's vacuous can-do lyric all butt awkwardly against Brooker's leisurely vocal. Though he tries to inject excitement into the choruses, it doesn't quite gel. For that matter, neither does the piano solo, in which he slams his palms on the keys and plays glissandos across them as if determined to add an edge to what otherwise is just slick radio fare.

'The Pursuit Of Happiness' (Brooker, Reid, Noble)
Reid's screed on the American dream is an awkward way to end an album by a band that had always managed to maintain its Britishness. The song swells and ebbs with hardly a ruffle, fading on the merest hint of military drumming that adds even more ambiguity to the words. You can't expect an immigrant to still write songs as pointed as 'Bringing Home The Bacon', but is America the reason for Reid's catalogue of moral and environmental decline, or is it the cure?

'Into The Flood' (Brooker, Reid, Noble)
Though a promotional CD of 'The Truth Won't Fade Away' was distributed to
the media in the US (along with its expensive video), only Germany released
the song as an actual single, pairing it with 'Learn To Fly' on the B-side,
and adding this album outtake on the maxi CD version. Esoteric Recordings
eventually placed it as a bonus track on the 2018 album reissue but labelled
it as a demo, which is surely true as it lacks all but the rudiments of the
sumptuous keyboards that are a characteristic of the album proper. It's a
pleasing but unexceptional rocker and mostly a feature for session guitarist
Bobby Mayo. The curious thing about this song is that it recycles verbatim
a lyric Reid had given to Robin Trower and Jack Bruce for their 1981 album
Truce, on which the lyric was set to a completely different tune and titled
'Gone Too Far'.

The Well's On Fire (2003)

Personnel:
Gary Brooker: piano, vocals
Mark Brzezicki: drums
Matthew Fisher: organ
Matt Pegg: bass
Geoff Whitehorn: guitar
Roger Taylor: vocals ('Shadow Boxed')
Recorded: October-November 2002, Cosford Mill Studios, Surrey, UK
Producers: Rafe McKenna, Procol Harum
Label: Eagle
Release date: March 2003
Charts: did not chart
Running time: 59:03

For the three decades after *The Prodigal Stranger*, Procol Harum was a viable concern, thanks largely to its back catalogue, which continued to attract fans and meant there were always plenty of bodies to fill a hall. Live albums were now the band's stock-in-trade. They released a large number of them, as both standard physical releases and fan-club downloads.

The rush of promotional work that followed *The Prodigal Stranger* saw a succession of lineups take the stage, including initial touring with guitarist Tim Renwick. By the end of 1991, guitar duties had passed to Geoff Whitehorn, and it's the Brooker/Fisher/Whitehorn/Bronze/Brzezicki lineup that did most of the heavy lifting for the next few years, even if it was hardly stable. Fisher was in and out in order to juggle his time with a computer science course at Cambridge. Brzezicki relinquished the stool to ex-King Crimson drummer Ian Wallace, and Fairport Convention stalwart Dave Pegg's son Matt took over on bass.

But after a high-profile 1995 UK tour capped by an orchestral concert at London's Barbican in 1996, the band again entered a period of hiatus. Brooker continued his side projects, only assembling the *Something Magic* band (without – of course – B. J. Wilson, but with Fisher and Cartwright) for the 1997 30th Anniversary Reunion Concert.

Finally, the *new* Procol Harum (Brooker, Fisher, Whitehorn, Pegg, and a returning Brzezicki) convened in 2001 for a short festival tour and another orchestral event. It was this version of the band that entered Roger Taylor's Cosford Mill Studios in October 2002 to record *The Well's On Fire* with Big Country producer Rafe McKenna. Eagle's press kit explained the rationale behind the album:

> *The Well's On Fire* opens Procol Harum's account for the new millennium and underlines the fact that the story, whose first pages were written back in the mid-1960s, is an ongoing one. During that time, some notable songs

slipped through the studio floorboards, and the original concept was to augment these with a few new compositions and thus 'tidy the closet'. But a creative period from lyricist Keith Reid – who favoured an all-new album – led to a different picture.

In the event, only two vintage songs saw release on the album: 'A Robe Of Silk' and 'So Far Behind'. The other 11 were more recent than *Something Magic*, and almost all were in Reid's new direct style of social commentary, which means they've dated far worse than his earlier work. The album title uses the burning Kuwaiti oil wells of the 1991 Gulf War as a symbol of the planet's economic and environmental collapse. (There's also surely a link to Bob Dylan's 'This Wheel's On Fire': a song about an out-of-control, approaching doom.) The resulting album was – again – extremely long and formatted for CD.

The Well's On Fire wasn't a hit, but that was par for the course. The computer graphics cover may well have turned off the curious, who'd expect to find an album even more shamelessly riding the latest fashions than the prior one did. Those who didn't recognize the band name wouldn't have bothered with it at all. But it started new rounds of live work and an ever-greater appreciation for the band as one of Britain's classic rock stalwarts.

In hindsight, it's indeed here that the main flow of the story ends, even if *The Well's On Fire* didn't quite 'tidy the closet'. Fisher was a stalwart during as many of the reunions and as much touring as his studies allowed, but he suddenly sundered his relationship with the band – understandably, for good – when he took Brooker to court in 2005. This was the last Procol Harum album Keith Reid wrote lyrics for, and it's something of a sour ending for a vision that had once been so singular. Nobody sounded like Reid in 1967. By 2003, he sounded like everybody else.

'An Old English Dream' (Brooker, Reid)

If you trace Bob Dylan's influences back before Woody Guthrie and the Beats, you eventually arrive at a swathe of European poets from W. H. Auden to Arthur Rimbaud. Auden's 1939 poem 'Refugee Blues' was one of a number in which the poet adopted the meter and phrasing of African-American song styles as a commentary on what was happening in Europe during the build towards World War II. In this case, the style equates German Jews fleeing persecution at home to the displaced and rootless slaves of the US. The poem's Biblical reportage style (I saw these significant things, and I dreamed these dire portents) was echoed in Dylan's 'A Hard Rain's A-Gonna Fall', and Reid references both Auden and Dylan in 'An Old English Dream', his own chronicle as a displaced, rootless Jew looking back toward the country he used to call home. It's a fine piece, less dogmatic than much of Reid's hectoring of the time, more nuanced and aching.

Brooker set the words to a strong rock ballad bedded on the things that had been sorely missing from *The Prodigal Stranger*: familiar acoustic and electric instruments played without too much electronic processing. The song begins on grand piano, just like the old days, and rises to a powerful refrain in which Brooker's voice (a little more roughened by age but still capable of soaring) spars with Whitehorn's guitar. There's no more pretension than this. It's a good song performed by a band to the best of their abilities to carry a powerful message.

'Shadow Boxed' (Brooker, Reid)

With its guitar judder, tuned percussion and insistent piano rhythm, 'Shadow Boxed' succeeds as an instantly attractive pop confection, though it lacks a melody strong enough to hook listeners. The merest touch of 1960s flower power suggests not nostalgia but sarcasm. Whitehorn is again the featured player, though his solo is no more than a climb up the frets and a wall of fuzz. The lyric is so lightweight that it sits uncomfortably against 'An Old English Dream'. Reid's been through a lot, the poor chap, but it's not clear here what the result of all these knocks has been. I guess he's still standing, and that's enough.

'A Robe Of Silk' (Brooker, Reid)

The first of the old songs was initially attempted during the earliest *Shine On Brightly* sessions in 1967. It's surprisingly tender and straightforward for Reid of the time – a love song in which the narrator promises to keep his partner safe through the Arabian-style dreams they'll have together. Brooker arranged the song faithfully to its age, including having Whitehorn play a facsimile of Robin Trower's guitar sound from 'The Milk Of Human Kindness' and Matthew Fisher reprise his trademark organ-playing. But it was an outtake for a reason, and the song never quite sparks.

'The Blink Of An Eye' (Brooker, Reid)

Though a New York City resident, Reid wasn't there during the terrorist attacks on 11 September 2001. He told UCLA Radio in February 2002:

> I was in London. In a weird sort of way, I wish I'd been there, especially as the part of Manhattan I live in is extremely close to the World Trade Center: seven blocks. And you know, I really felt for the people that I knew in the area. I had to write a song about it, and a friend of mine is setting it to music. That's one of the lucky things about being a writer: you have some outlet for when these terrible things happen.

The date of the interview – months ahead of *The Well's On Fire* – suggests the 'friend of mine' was somebody other than Gary Brooker or that Reid was forbidden from mentioning the new Procol Harum work just yet. His lyric is outraged reportage, as you'd expect, but painfully superficial. He writes of 'a big black bird' swooping on the city and how 'the dreams of so many have gone up in smoke'. There's no deeper engagement than this. The refrain – 'We thought we were living on easy street/But they pulled the rug from under our feet' – is utterly inadequate, particularly from a writer who could channel Auden and Dylan to express the heartfelt emotions of 'An Old English Dream'. Instead, all the song's power is expressed in Brooker's voice, turning a slight work into real heartache.

'The VIP Room' (Brooker, Reid)
Reid so sets himself up for a critical drubbing with what on the surface is a celebration of being rich ('If I'm eating pie, I want the best silver plate') that the only way to excuse the song is to assume it's all bluff. The trouble is, it's hard to tell. The line I just quoted sounds a lot like 'Grand Hotel'. In the press kit that accompanied *The Well's On Fire*, Reid claimed the song has 'real New York attitude', and there certainly are culturally clumsy word choices, like 'goons', 'croak', and 'poontang', that suggest he's putting on a voice. Brooker plays along, matching the lyric to swaggering rock and singing in a gruff drawl that adds a bluesman's strut throughout.

'The Question' (Fisher, Reid)
You have to go back a very long way to find another Fisher/Reid song. There are only two, both on *A Salty Dog*: 'Wreck Of The Hesperus' and 'Pilgrim's Progress'. Unlike the experiments of those songs, this is a straightforward soft-rock groove that slips along for five minutes, hardly rousing for Whitehorn's guitar solo and Fisher's brief organ feature. The words aren't challenging, either. They simply warn an unknown protagonist to be sure he's blameless before pointing the finger at others.

'This World Is Rich (For Stephen Maboe)' (Brooker, Reid)
Here's some of that finger-pointing: a relatively wealthy Western man quoting the struggles of the black poor as if they were his own. It's much of a piece with 'Holding On' from *The Prodigal Stranger* or 'Memorial Drive' from *Broken Barricades*. Reid's inspiration was the John Vidal article 'Great Trek from the Slums to the Promised Land' from *The Guardian* on 2 September 2002. It documented a 2002 local protest march to the World Summit on Sustainable Development in Sandtown, South Africa. Vidal equated the march to the wider problems the poor face in society: 'To reach the rich world, the poor must go 'round in circles and be diverted by roadblocks at every point'. He quoted protestor Stephen Maboe from Sasolburg: 'This world is rich, but it is not mine. I am not angry that they have so much and we have so little, but I want people to know our position. Where I live, the air pollution is terrible and the poverty is intense. The rich get richer; the poor get poorer. What must we do?'. The lyric repeats Maboe's words faithfully, Reid adding commentary of his own as if spoken in Maboe's voice. It's undeniably potent as a message, and Brooker set it sensitively, not as a protest anthem but as a

small and personal testimony, even if he couldn't resist a few African motifs similar to those he used in 'Holding On'.

'Fellow Travellers' (Fisher, Reid)
The second Fisher/Reid song on *The Well's On Fire* has much more to commend it than 'The Question'. Fisher was forthright that he stole the tune from the 1711 Handel opera *Rinaldo,* explaining in the press kit: 'It's a beautiful aria from an opera, called 'Laschia ch'io pianga'. I'm being quite upfront about borrowing it, but I don't think Handel wants his royalties'.

 With its leisurely tempo, classical theme, and hymn-like verses, 'Fellow Travellers' is consciously in the same style as early Procol Harum ballads, though there's little prominent organ. Instead, Whitehorn plays a solo while Fisher contributes a wash of Hammond chords and swoops.

'Wall Street Blues' (Brooker, Reid)
Following on from 'This World Is Rich', this lyric sneers at the investors whose wealth tumbled in the stock market downturn of 2002. There's zero sympathy in 'Wall Street Blues': Reid merely delights in their broken dreams. Nor can Brooker summon a jot of kinship with them, growling the song in the same way as 'The VIP Room'.

'The Emperor's New Clothes' (Brooker, Reid)
Brooker's sorrowful piano adds a surprising touch of empathy here, even though Reid's lyric is one of the harshest on the album. He piles into the US political apparatus, castigating the 'manic delusion' and 'self-serving lies' of the candidates and the greed of the machinery they perpetuate. Not all of it rings true – 'The only person you fool is yourself' was out of touch then and is more so now, and the message in the refrain that 'everyone knows' the emperor is naked glosses over the *need* to believe and the sincere trust in their leaders on both sides of the political divide. It's surprising that Reid couldn't give the song more nuance. And Brooker's treatment – excellent though it is – has no hope of adding depth.

'So Far Behind' (Brooker, Reid)
You can tell by the opening line, 'Your convent-cloistered cluttered mind', that this is an old song: an outtake from *Procol's Ninth* at the latest. But the treatment is modern, skipping around in the same bright pop space as 'Shadow Boxed'. Fisher has fun with his organ lines, and Brooker tries hard to enthuse the others. But Whitehorn plays another uninspired solo, and a long closing section merely counts off the seconds.

'Every Dog Will Have His Day' (Brooker, Fisher, Reid)
This is an R&B romp with dog noises and some witty lines ('When a puppy chews its balls/Lord, you know you've met your match') but not much in the

way of a melody or message. Fisher again came up with the basic idea, and it would be fun to know exactly what his version consisted of before Brooker turned it into the Paramounts-style rave-up we hear here.

'Weisselklenzenacht (The Signature)' (Fisher)
It's fitting that the final track is credited to Fisher, who also contributed music to the final piece on each of the Procol Harum albums he appeared on in the 1960s. That's another circle joined, more so since the instrumental is a reimagining of 'Repent Walpurgis' right down to its Germanic-sounding title. The organ even starts with an all-too-familiar texture. It is widescreen and triumphant, culminating in a sculptural Whitehorn solo that hits all the expected highs. But it's also curiously empty, an exercise in hollow self-reverence.

Novum (2017)

Personnel:
Gary Brooker: piano, accordion, vocals
Geoff Dunn: drums
Matt Pegg: bass, vocals
Josh Phillips: keyboards, vocals
Geoff Whitehorn: guitar, vocals
Recorded: October-December 2016, Angelic Studios, Northampton; Rimshot
Studios, Kent, UK
Producer: Dennis Weinreich
Label: Eagle
Release date: April 2017
Charts: did not chart
Running time: 56:08

If it was a purposeful decision for Brooker not to work with Reid on this
album but collaborate with fine English lyricist Pete Brown, that would
have made sense in terms of publicity since Brown's involvement was the
thing reviewers most wanted to write about. Equally, this had to be a Procol
Harum release rather than a Gary Brooker solo album, regardless of who was
driving the pen, since it could then be married to the band's 50th anniversary.
Brooker told *Prog* in 2018:

> There were other things going on – personal things, people being ill, and
> court cases. So, the atmosphere didn't inspire me to go and do Procol. I
> think Reid lost interest quite a long time ago. I spoke to Pete Brown about
> it two years ago. I knew Pete from when he was doing Cream, and he just
> said, 'If you're ever thinking of doing something, bear me in mind. I'd love to
> contribute'. He does what he wants to do but admires Keith Reid and knows
> that you have to have a certain kind of lyric if it's going to be a Procol song.

In 2017, Brooker told *Classic Rock* he could hardly contain his resentment
toward Reid, particularly when it came to Reid's function as road manager
in the early years, with Brooker wondering why he was in the entourage: 'At
some point after the last album, we came to a crossroads. He turned left and I
went straight on. There's not a lot more I can say about it than that. I would say
that it was extremely disappointing that we haven't seen this thing through to
our dying day. There are so many questions in the aftermath, like why was he
there? Moral support, maybe. But there's always people who do that'.

Brown's flexibility was something Brooker mentioned repeatedly to
interviewers, almost as if Brown was a breath of fresh air after decades of
Reid's dour, rigid pronouncements. Brooker told *Shindig* in 2018: 'We hooked
up after Keith Reid retired. Pete offered to do some lyrics for me and is very
amenable, happy to adapt things to my style'.

Ironically, Brown explained that *Novum* was *intended* to be an album of dour, rigid pronouncements. He told *Songfacts* in 2017: 'I had met Gary a couple of times, but I didn't know him at all. When they were thinking about a new record, they thought about me doing it. So they put us together and Gary and I had a very brief meeting. I said, 'Got any ideas for a theme?' and he said, 'Yeah, Ten Commandments'. We drifted way away from that, but there are elements in there that were inspired by the idea'.

The game when listening to *Novum* is to match each of the songs to one of the commandments, though, as Brown says, it's clear that not every song is slotted into the concept.

After uninspiring covers on the previous two studio albums, *Novum* finally had one that nodded back to the old work. Julia Brown's illustration feels like a mix of Dickinson's first LP and the George Underwood version of *Shine On Brightly* while nodding subtly to *Exotic Birds And Fruit*. Brooker admitted to *Classic Rock* that he didn't like it: 'It's been a bit of a bone of contention. There's been a few discussions. I mean, I can see what Julia is doing. The girl looks a little more wispy, but she's surrounded by a little more comfort and luxury. Anyway, we move on. I expect I'll get a free T-shirt of it, and then I may change my mind'. He must have done just that, as the 2018 box set *Still There'll Be More* had much the same design, and by the same artist.

'I Told On You' (Brooker, Phillips, Brown)
Novum begins unpromisingly with mid-tempo commercial rock that coasts almost entirely on Brooker's familiar voice. Whitehorn takes the solo but doesn't have enough space to explore the groove. Brown's lyric is a rejection of someone who set themselves up as king of a relationship. He told *Songfacts*: 'Originally, I sketched out a lot of these things quite a long time ago, and then time passed by and then we eventually got down to it. 'I Told On You' seems now to be about Brexit and some of the stuff that's happened because of that, but that was completely unintentional at the time'.

In truth, there's little in the song that could be construed as referring to the 2016 referendum. One curious mention of Dover is as much as we get.

'Last Chance Motel' (Brooker, Phillips, Brown)
Brown's lyric is a salutary warning against infidelity. The narrator explains that his best friend's wife was so tempting that he was soon 'breaking that big law' with her at the motel of the title. (*She* breaks the adultery Commandment. *He* covets his neighbour's ox.) Eventually, they're exposed, and the best friend beats up the narrator and gives the woman 'a bullet between those big blue eyes'. Whatever the actual morality on offer, three lives are wrecked because of the affair, and one of these people learns a lesson that seems a little harsh. Brooker presents the story as a heartfelt power ballad, flavoured with big harmony vocals and keyboards sounding like a string section.

'Image Of The Beast' (Brooker, Phillips, Whitehorn, Brown)
Brown's damnation of greed (a deadly sin, not a Commandment) differs little
from that of his predecessor's 'All Our Dreams Are Sold' on *The Prodigal
Stranger* and is played in the same gruff blues style as 'The VIP Room' on
The Well's On Fire. Here's the TV again: master of our homes. Here also
are the naked emperor and 'creepy priests', all of them simply conduits to
siphon away our hard-earned money. But Brown claimed his inspiration was
something quite different, as he told *Songfacts*: 'There's a terrific book by the
American science fiction writer Philip José Farmer. It's very, very fantastical
and very bizarre, and it's called *Image Of The Beast*. I got some ideas out of
that. I'm a big science fiction fan'. Let's assume Brown was teasing. *Image
Of The Beast* (first published by erotic-fiction imprint Essex House in 1968)
is actually a transgressive horror novel about shapeshifting monsters having
bizarre sex in gothic chambers.

'Soldier' (Brooker, Phillips)
This is the first of only two lyrics Brooker ever wrote for Procol Harum. As
you'd expect, it's a condemnation of war, as seen through the eyes of a soldier
sick of fighting. Brooker's dazed resignation is masterfully matched to the
music: a world-burdened ballad.

'Don't Get Caught' (Brooker, Phillips, Brown)
Sequencing two similar ballads one after the other feels clumsy, especially
since this one doesn't have the power of 'Soldier'. It repeats the female
harmony vocals and strings sound from 'Last Chance Motel', but Brooker
strains to bring the required intensity to his voice in the refrain. Brown's lyric
is little more than the title suggests, and it feels a lot like this was originally
intended as the album finale.

'Neighbour' (Brooker, Phillips, Brown)
This admonition against envy is a welcome change of pace to upbeat Cajun-
flavoured folk-rock reminiscent of latter-day Bob Dylan. It tries hard to be quirky,
even having the same nod to 'Entrance Of The Gladiators' as ''Twas Teatime At
The Circus'. But if we take Brooker's word for it, this disguises a genuine
animosity. In 2017, he told *Classic Rock* about the laughter at the end of the
track: 'What wasn't there was a gun – a starting pistol actually – that I had in the
studio, that I fired right at the end of the song. Nobody knew I had it. I was
singing about my neighbour, who I hate. I really wish him ill. So I fired this pistol
right next to the microphone, and then I started to laugh because it sounded like
a cap gun going off. It didn't record very well. So that got taken out'.

'Sunday Morning' (Brooker, Phillips, Brown)
A commiseration of the working man's lot, 'Sunday Morning' is of note
for incorporating musical touches from 'Magdalene' on *Shine On Brightly*,

including its Salvation Army drumming. Brown explained to *Songfacts*: 'It's got a bit of a spirit there. It's slightly gospely the way that Gary phrased it. It's about a working-class person who does what he does and works hard and plays hard'.

The message of the song is that on Sunday morning (his one precious moment of freedom from toil), the labourer doesn't need or wish to go to church since 'Every minute's more holy to me'.

'Businessman' (Brooker, Phillips, Brown)
Brown's lyric describes the opposite of the previous song: an unscrupulous company climber who *does* go to church, though 'I think that just makes things worse'. There's not much fire in these words, but Brooker sets them to the album's most muscular rock arrangement.

'Can't Say That' (Brooker, Phillips, Brown)
The band's longest singleton at 7:11 might edge out 'Whaling Stories' to the title but has nothing of the earlier track's invention. It's merely a boogie workout, which finally gives Whitehorn the space for a substantial solo. Brown essentially rewrites 'Butterfly Boys' for the album's fourth character study in a row: a manager with all the graces of a mob boss.

'The Only One' (Brooker, Phillips, Brown)
Brooker's plaintive piano ballad frames Brown's most curious lyric on the album – a God's-eye view of creation ('It was just an accident'), scant justification for divine wrath, and an uncomfortably dismissive attitude toward humanity ('Some say I've gone and left you/But I was never really there'). All this is balanced by a swelling refrain in which the assertion 'I am in your head' is open to two contradictory readings: God is everywhere, or God is a figment of our imagination. Brown told *Songfacts*: 'I'm not sure about Gary, but I'm absolutely not religious at all. I grew up Jewish, but not having any particular regard for religion or gods or anything. So, I'm on the other side of the coin'. It sets up a fascinating disconnect: Brooker singing with soulful sincerity what could be a rejection of his own beliefs.

'Somewhen' (Brooker)
If the God of 'The Only One' is in doubt, then Brooker's second lyric closes the band's final album on a small and very human certainty: the writer's love for his wife. It's poignantly humble, just Brooker's ageing voice straining to perform a delicate hymn-like melody against unadorned grand piano.

'Missing Persons (Alive Forever)' (2021)

Personnel:
Gary Brooker: piano, vocals
Geoff Dunn: drums
Matt Pegg: bass
Josh Phillips: organ
Geoff Whitehorn: guitar
Written by: Brooker, Reid
Producer: Procol Harum
Label: Esoteric Antenna
Release date: May 2021 (UK only)
Charts: did not chart
Running time: 5:36

Had the quiet dignity of 'Somewhen' been the last we'd heard from Gary
Brooker, then *Novum* would be a fitting valedictory. Whether he liked it or
not, it was a time of winding down, of inevitable endings, and of wrapping
up what was still left to wrap up. The band had kept going over the past two
decades, and there were still highs (most notably a return to the Isle Of Wight
festival in 2006) and the ever-compelling orchestral extravaganzas. But an
attempted mugging in South Africa in 2012, when Brooker was dosed with
Rohypnol in a bar and passed out on the way back to his hotel, left him with
permanent injuries, including the loss of hearing in his left ear. A serious
fall during a performance at the Royal Festival Hall in 2017 gave him more
head injuries. That we had *Novum* at all from a man who was 71 at the time
of its recording and ought to be retired was a miracle, let alone that he kept
on touring doggedly. He didn't cease playing live until 2019, after which the
Covid-19 lockdown stole away anything else he might have done. Surely,
there would have been more concerts. Finally, cancer took Brooker in 2022
and it took both Reid and Brown a year later.

During the pandemic, one last physical release crept out, largely
unnoticed and almost immediately forgotten. On the surface, the CD-only
single 'Missing Persons (Alive Forever)' appeared to be a reunion with
Keith Reid. But it wasn't a new song at all, having been performed live as
early as 2007, and it was a setting of words that Brooker might have had
in his possession much earlier. It certainly predated Brown's involvement.
Little more is known about it. Esoteric Antenna's press release claimed that
Brooker had stumbled upon two outtakes (this song and the B-side 'War
is Not Healthy') and decided to complete them, presumably in his home
studio. They quoted him as saying: 'They weren't written last week, neither
are they old. Keith Reid's lyrics sound incredibly apt for the time we're
living in. This is the sound of Procol Harum today'. The addition of a 'radio
edit' (a minute shorter) of 'Missing Persons' enabled Esoteric to market the
release as an EP, but it's not really that.

'Missing Persons' is a song about separation: mother from child, friends that drifted away, those sundered for good by bereavement, and public figures who have passed into memory. Had Brooker known he was dying of cancer in 2021, he would surely have considered it a tribute to his lost partnership with a man who'd shared the joys and sorrows of his professional life since they first met as green writers in 1966: a reaching out to Reid, and a turning down of the light. There's certainly the sense that the song wraps up the Procol Harum sound. Prominent Hammond organ flavours the piece throughout, played by Josh Phillips in conscious imitation of Matthew Fisher's classical style. There was no hope the single could be commercially successful, but that wasn't the point.

'War Is Not Healthy' (Brooker, Reid)
Did there need to be a B-side at all? Reid's lyric simply spits pacifist slogans inspired by artist Lorraine Schneider's 1966 painting 'War Is Not Healthy For Children And Other Living Things'. The song is a strident and not entirely convincing marching anthem, and it feels so wrong to end here. Instead, let's leave the last word to Brooker from an interview with *Prog* in 2017:

> The only reason I would go on stage with Procol Harum, or make a record as Procol Harum, is because I think we've always had – I don't know what the right expression is – a bit of dignity in there, certain standards of music. To keep a standard going that amount of time – which, although a lot of British people don't know it, we have done – is an achievement in itself.

Beyond These Things

This book documents only the standard studio albums and singles released by Procol Harum, along with *Procol Harum Live*, which it would have been absurd to omit, and they're far from the full story. A huge number of outtakes, alternate mixes, and edits are available on expanded CD versions of much of the band's catalogue: many of them are revelatory. There are also songs that were performed live but never made it to the studio, including a reworking of Procol Harum highlights 'Last Train To Niagara', officially released from a performance at Irvine Meadows Amphitheatre, California, in 1993.

There have been two lavish box sets mixing studio classics, rarities, live work and footage: *All This And More...* (2009) and *Still There'll Be More* (2018). But to date, there's no comprehensive packaging of the full breadth of the band's work, and gaps remain in the official record. In particular, few of the promotional appearances and films that the band produced have been released. For example, there's no official nod to the promotional film they made for 'A Whiter Shade Of Pale' rather than play *Top Of The Pops* yet again during the chaos of its run at the top of the charts. The BBC rejected the film because it included Vietnam footage.

In 1970, an excellent 50-minute Australian TV documentary traced the band's career to that point through revealing and perceptive interviews and unique performances, including candid footage of them stomping around a snowy English countryside, playing darts in a pub (Wilson downs a pint in seconds), looning around in a zoo, and Trower narrowly avoiding death on a railway-station platform. It's the best place to see Keith Reid (who sure does need a cuddle), but you'll have to stray out of official sources to view it.

There's much better official documentation of the band's radio and TV sessions. They stretch right back to the Royer/Harrison lineup. Bootlegs exist of the band live from as early as August 1967, but the first official record of how Procol Harum sounded on stage is 20 minutes 'live in the USA' first released on the *40 Years* edition of *A Salty Dog* in 2009, and dated only to April 1969. It's actually a performance at Fillmore West.

Procol Harum played the Isle of Wight festival in 1970, sandwiched between Family and The Voices of East Harlem late on Friday night, but they didn't appear in the movie *Message To Love*. The only sanctioned audio records of their participation are 'A Salty Dog' on the compilation *The First Great Rock Festivals Of The Seventies* (1971) (never officially reissued on vinyl or released on CD) and 'Juicy John Pink' on *All This And More...*, which the band stomps through largely to keep themselves and the audience warm.

There is official audio of the Hollywood Bowl concert from 21 September 1973 (a big deal at the time), performed with the Los Angeles Philharmonic and the Roger Wagner Chorale and recorded for D.I.R. Broadcasting's *King Biscuit Flower Hour*. Three tracks were extracted for *All This And More...*, and the entire 54-minute tape was included in *Still There'll Be More*.

Procol Harum get 12 minutes on the commemorative LP *Over The Rainbow* that documented the final concert at the Rainbow Theatre in London on 16 March 1975 before the venue closed for renovation. They play 'Grand Hotel' (interpolating a solo Brooker rendition of 'Over The Rainbow'), and they back gravelly singer Frankie Miller on 'Brickyard Blues'. The former was released on the 2004 CD edition of *Grand Hotel* but hasn't been seen since.

As you'd expect, much more live material exists of the reformed bands from 1991 onwards. Official physical and download-only releases – both audio and DVD – include *One More Time – Live In Utrecht 1992*, *Live In Copenhagen 2001*, *Live At The Union Chapel* (London 2003), *Live At Ledreborg* (2006, also released as *In Concert With The Danish National Concert Orchestra And Choir*), *One Eye To The Future* (Italy 2007), *Spirit Of Nøkken* (mostly St. Petersburg 2009), *MMX* (mostly from various European locations in 2010, *Some Long Road* (various dates in 2012 and 2013), and *The One & Only One* (UK 2017).

Procol Harum completists will want the music of The Paramounts, which is surely the only reason it's been anthologised in the 60 years since. Sixteen of the band's tracks were released as the LP *Whiter Shades Of R&B* in 1983, and 22 as *The Paramounts At Abbey Road* in 1998, but in truth, there's nothing special about them. However, in 1969, when Procol Harum found themselves as a performing group consisting *entirely* of members who'd been in The Paramounts, they began to lean on the old band's repertoire to loosen up in the studio. We have one official memento of the jams: a 1970 track listed as 'Rockin' Warm-up/Go Go Go (Move On Down The Line)' on the 1999 release *Home...Plus*.

A commercial enterprise, such as a rock group on a strict budget, won't spend time in the studio unless there's a good reason to, particularly a band with finances as perilous as Procol Harum's. Nevertheless, by the end of the *Home* sessions, Chris Thomas found himself overseeing an entire extra album's worth of these old R&B and soul songs: 'High School Confidential', 'Kansas City', 'Lucille', 'Matchbox', 'The Girl Can't Help It' and more. A little premature – you'd think – for guys in their early 20s to relive their youth, but Brooker, for one, had been in the business for nearly a decade, and this music was his life. Besides, back-to-basics was very much the zeitgeist in Britain in 1970, led by bands like The Move and The Who, and was soon to mutate into glam. And the recording limitations aside, in every way, the sessions stand up significantly better than John Lennon's own trawl through his youth, *Rock 'N' Roll*, which he began recording in 1973. Ten years later, you could have put Jeff Lynne's name on Procol Harum's 'Old Black Joe' and it would have been a hit.

Given that *Home* had a cover design made for a gatefold, there's the possibility that the band intended the recordings to occupy a second bonus disc. But they languished until 1997, when they were released as *Ain't Nothin' To Get Excited About* under the pseudonym *Liquorice John Death*, with a vinyl-friendly running time of 39:27.

There's an even-odder item in the band's catalogue. In August 1995, Brooker put together *The Long Goodbye: The Symphonic Music Of Procol Harum*: an album of orchestral versions of Procol Harum songs. This was one of a small vogue in orchestral reimaginings at the time, which also included *Symphonic Music Of Yes* (1993), *Symphonic Music Of The Rolling Stones* (1994) and *Symphonic Music Of The Who* (1998). Brooker told *Progression* in 1996:

> BMG Classics asked me if I'd help them do *The Symphonic Music of Procol Harum*. It's not a Procol Harum album; it mainly features the London Symphony Orchestra. We did brand new orchestrations for about a dozen songs. It was originally meant to be a classical record, but they ended up wanting a bit of crossover in it, I think. So, two or three songs have drums and guitar on them as well. James Galway plays flute, and we've got a classical singer doing 'Grand Hotel'.

That classical singer was Jerry Hadley. There were also the celebrity arrangers Nicholas Dodd, Christian Kabitz, and Curved Air's Darryl Way. Procol Harum members Dave Bronze and Mark Brzezicki play on most of the pieces, while Trower and Fisher convene for a version of 'Repent Walpurgis'. The title track is not a Procol Harum song at all, but one from Brooker's solo album *Echoes In The Night*. But the most surprising choice, and the aspect that may make Procol Harum fans think twice about picking up the album, is the decision to relinquish Brooker's vocal duties on 'Simple Sister' to Tom Jones. In fairness, he's rather good. Brooker told *Progression*:

> Tom was walking past the studio, and I said, 'Tom, come in and check this out. Would you like to sing one on here?' and he said he'd love to. So I gave him about five songs with my guide vocals on them. He took them away that night and came back the next day. He hadn't had much time, I think. He couldn't do the more complicated ones, which he really didn't know. So we went for the easy ones. 'Simple Sister' by Tom Jones is somewhat of a landmark in my calendar.

It wasn't an isolated incident. In 1996, Brooker organized a live concert in aid of his local church, released as the album *Within Our House*. He sings a clutch of old Procol Harum songs ('A Salty Dog, 'A Whiter Shade Of Pale') alongside a choir, string quartet, and a small band including Bronze and Brzezicki. The title track was a new Brooker/Reid song that has not been released elsewhere.